UPSIDE UP

Real Estate Investing:

Successful Strategies to
Make Money in *Any* Market

OR

How to Locate, Finance, and Purchase
Residential Rental Property, Create Value and
Residual Income for Retirement, and Reduce
Your Income Taxes, All in Your Spare Time

Bob Zachmeier

Out of the Box Books
Tucson, Arizona

Copyright © 2008 by Bob Zachmeier

ISBN: 978-0-9801855-0-8

Library of Congress Control Number:
2007909766

For information on other books by Bob Zachmeier
visit the publisher's website at:
www.outoftheboxbooks.com

When it comes to books… think Out of the Box!

Out of the Box Books
P.O. Box 64878, Tucson, AZ 85728

For BettyJo Zachmeier and Camille Zachmeier, my mom and my wife. Each has had a profound and positive influence on my life. My mother instilled in me the confidence to challenge the norm. My wife inspires me to do just that and to share with others what we learn along the way.

"The road to success is filled with women pushing their husbands along." – Thomas R. Dewar

Table of Contents

TABLE OF CONTENTS

TABLE OF CONTENTS

TABLE OF CONTENTS

TABLE OF CONTENTS

TABLE OF CONTENTS

Upside Up™ *in Real Life* (Actual Experiences)

TABLE OF CONTENTS

Upside Up™ in Real Life (Actual Experiences)

TABLE OF CONTENTS

Tables in This Book

ACKNOWLEDGEMENTS

I can't say enough about the help I've received from those around me to complete this book. When I started the initial outline five years ago I had no idea of the work that it would take before seeing the finished product in print.

Progress was painfully slow when I first started putting the words on paper. The perfectionist in me kept wanting to go back to rephrase each sentence before I'd even completed a paragraph. Then I took a course on writing from Tom Bird at Pima Community College in Tucson, Arizona.

I learned that you need to write early in the morning before drinking any coffee or waking up your "logical, critical mind," or *left brain*. This is the analytical side of your brain that second-guesses everything that you do, and mine was doing its job very well.

In the *natural* state, your "creative, connected mind," or *right brain*, connects with your pen and you can't seem to get the words written fast enough. This was the solution to my writing problem!

So, I wrote the majority of this text on index cards while sitting in a lawn chair in my back yard between the hours of four o'clock and six o'clock in the morning *without any coffee!*

I could never have completed this project without the help and support of many others, so let me thank them here.

I thank God for the love and support of my wife, Camille, who endured countless nights of being awakened when I came to bed well after midnight, or when I got up early to write. She even spent entire *days* alone on our vacations, while I edited, revised, and re-edited the developing manuscript.

ACKNOWLEDGEMENTS

My dad taught me to see things as they *could be* rather than seeing them as they are. His *vision* and my mother's optimism are alive and well in me. Although my dad passed away in 1996, my mother is still actively experiencing life. She helped out a lot on this book by proofreading the completed chapters during her visits to see us. Computer spell checking programs miss a lot of errors, but Mom sure doesn't!

It's said that God places people in your life when you need them most, and that was the case with Robert Merideth, my editor and friend. We met when Robert took my real estate investing class at the college. In all my years of teaching, he's the only student to give *me* homework each week!

At first, I didn't know what to think of his analytical nature, but I can assure you that I've learned a lot more from him than I can ever expect to teach. Robert's gentle nudges and suggestions have been responsible for a lot of content being added to this book that I hadn't even considered. His patience and commitment to helping me complete this project is the only reason you're reading it now.

Writing a book consumes most of the time you have to do other things. I can't thank John Harings enough for his encouragement, friendship, and for "picking up the slack" to help Camille keep our real estate business running while I was entrenched in this effort.

I'd like to also thank the friends and family members who have invested with me over the years, including: Bill and BettyJo Zachmeier, Mike Zachmeier, Gary Peightal, George Yinemen, Mike and Jody Herk, Rich and Michelle Allen, Christian and Michelle Hasselberg, Rusty and Birgit Owens, Scott and Susan Pope, Russ and Tamyra Althof, Stuart and Lynette Lott, and the thirty members of EGG, our private bank.

ACKNOWLEDGEMENTS

Many of the experiences in this book would not have happened without each of us trusting one another implicitly with large sums of money. I've heard it said that friends and money don't mix, but whoever said that doesn't know *my* friends.

A team is only as good as its players. I owe many of my real estate successes to the friendship and advice I receive from my professional team including my accountant, Sean McCoy, my attorney, Jim Whitehill, and my escrow officer, Joann Bersell.

I'd also like to thank Marianne Kartsonis, my assistant, who diligently converted many of my scribbled index cards to electronic text and David Miner at Pima Community College who for the past eight years, has worked around my personal commitments when scheduling the investment classes I teach.

As a life-long learner, I'm always looking for new ideas. My investment horizons have been vastly widened by Alan and Joan Langston, founders of the Arizona Real Estate Investor's Association (AZREIA).

My view of the real estate business has been changed forever by Craig Proctor's Quantum Leap System. Our real estate coaches, Craig Proctor, Todd Walters, and Danny Griffin are the best real estate minds in the world. Their coaching over the past three years has helped us take a *quantum leap* with our real estate business to levels I couldn't have imagined possible before meeting them.

Last, but not least, I'd like to thank the friends and family members who've helped to critique the many drafts of this book for missing content and typographical errors. This has truly been a team effort, and I appreciate all of the help!

INTRODUCTION

In 1982 I started investing in real estate without clearly defined goals or much planning; I was 22-years old and possessed only ambition and desire. During several years of trying different investment strategies, I made several mistakes.

These experiences were invaluable because I learned which investment strategies work and which ones don't. More importantly, I learned *why* the strategies work or don't work.

The knowledge shared in this book represents more than 25 years of education from the school of "hard knocks." To avoid the mistakes I've made, read this book, learn the basics of investing, establish a plan, and follow it to the letter. If you do this, you'll find success much faster than I did. It's never too late to become a successful real estate investor.

It's taken years to perfect my investing process and create a systematic approach for investing that avoids my past failures and repeats all of the successes. My *Upside Up*™ system is not only profitable and repeatable; it works in both buyer's and seller's markets.

More than thirty stories of my personal mistakes and triumphs are sprinkled throughout this book in text boxes with the heading: *Upside Up*™ *In Real Life*. A list of these experiences is provided in the Table of Contents.

Those who purchase investment properties through our real estate company are taught how to follow this system. Within a few months of buying their first investment property, most of our clients either refinance or sell their completed project. The most common reaction to the five-digit "paycheck" they receive from the title company is, "let's do it again!"

1

Lessons to
Learn From

"Challenges are what make life interesting; overcoming them is what makes life meaningful."– Joshua J. Marine

A Tax Problem Develops

After graduating from college in 1980, I took a job as an instrument engineer on a seismic exploration crew. The quest to locate underground oil and gas reserves took me all over the western United States during the summer months and to the North Slope of Alaska in the winter.

My pay more than doubled in Alaska due to the extreme 30-degrees-below-zero temperatures, 24 hours of darkness, and 18-hour work days. At the age of 21, I was earning nearly $10,000 per *month* during those frigid Alaskan winters. Because all of my living expenses were paid by my employer, I was able to send my entire paycheck home to my mother, who would deposit it into my savings account.

After deductions for income tax, Social Security, and medical and dental insurance, my take home pay was slightly over *half* of my gross pay. It just didn't seem fair that I only received half of my pay after working such long days in a very cold and unfriendly environment, far away from family, friends, and civilization. So I decided to do something about it.

Buying My First Properties

I purchased my first investment property, a brand new condominium, in June 1982. I'd read several books about the tax benefits of owning real estate, and decided to reduce my tax burden by buying rental property. At the time, there was a lot of news about the double-digit appreciation occurring in California. By investing 10% of the purchase price as a down payment, you could earn over 100% per year! (Assuming the appreciation remained 10% or more). I was excited about the millions of dollars I was about to make.

The 18% interest rates on loans at the time were not a deterrent to me. I found a first-time homebuyer program to get my interest rate on the condo down to 15 ¼% and I felt *lucky!*

Because the rent was lower than my mortgage payment, HOA fee, and other expenses, I had a *negative cash flow* of nearly $500 per month. Still, I was confident that appreciation would easily outpace the deficit I was paying out of pocket.

The next month, I purchased a second property, a thirty-year-old duplex. I was able to assume the seller's loan with an interest rate of only 7% (a very low rate at the time).

Due to the low mortgage payment, the rental income on this property was higher than my expenses, so this property produced a *positive cash flow* of about $110 per month.

Building Rental Property

In 1983, I formed a partnership with three friends from college. We'd all landed good-paying jobs, but I was the only one who had any income tax deductions. We decided to invest in real estate as a group for the tax deductions. To avoid the pitfalls I'd experienced from *buying* rental properties, we decided to *build* rental properties.

We formed a partnership and located a vacant lot in Bismarck, the capital of my home state of North Dakota. Our land was located a few blocks from two hospitals, so we determined that we'd have a rental base of medical personnel who could easily walk to either hospital from our location.

We hired a builder to construct a two-story, four-unit apartment building. Since my partners and I all lived out-of-state, my mother was kind enough to oversee the construction and make all of the decisions about cabinets, appliances, paint colors, and so on. She also kept the contractor in line during the construction process. Mom did such a great job for us during the construction of the building, we hired her to be our property manager.

We were each 23-years old and collectively we owned a beautiful new building that was rented (to our delight) to mostly nurses. Due to the high interest rates at the time, this property also produced a negative cash flow each month. While we'd achieved our goal of creating a great tax write off, the amount of money we received as income-tax credits was only offsetting a small portion of the money we lost each month due to the rent being lower than our expenses.

Several years later, one of my partners was transferred to Bismarck and expressed an interest in buying the building from the rest of us.

The negative cash flow each month had gotten old, especially since we had imagined getting rich from our investment. So, one by one, we each sold our respective shares for, as it turned out, less than what we'd invested in the property. Our partner refinanced the property a few times as interest rates declined, but he and his wife still own that building today!

Investment Results

All of the properties I'd purchased to this point were within seven miles of Mandan, North Dakota, where I'd grown up. I chose this location because I was familiar with the area and because my parents—who had agreed to manage the properties while I was working out of state—lived nearby.

Several years after purchasing these "money-losing" investment properties, while helping my parents move, I accidentally dropped the "N" volume of the *World Book*

Encyclopedia. The book fell open to "North Dakota" and it was then that I noticed that the population of the state had been decreasing steadily for several years. This little tidbit of information would come back to haunt me when I began to sell my properties many years later.

In 1996, I sold the duplex for two-thousand dollars more than I'd paid for it in 1982. My accountant had established a 15-year depreciation schedule for the property and 14 of the years had transpired.

During this time, I'd paid off more than one-third of the loan balance, but the property had been depreciated to the point that all but $4,000 of the sale price was determined to be a taxable "gain." After the sale, I walked out of the title company office with a very nice check, but had to pay every penny of it to the IRS the following April for income taxes.

The next year, I received an offer to buy my condo. This property had to be handled differently because I'd refinanced it twice and still owed a substantial amount on the loan. This property had been totally depreciated during the fifteen previous tax years. The equity in this property was thousands of dollars short of what I'd need to pay the taxes, so I couldn't afford to sell it!

I began thinking of "out-of-the-box" ways to avoid having to bring money to the closing table in order to sell my "investment." After much research, I found that my college would take properties as endowments as long as there wasn't a mortgage on them. I convinced a college representative to come to the closing, even though I did have a mortgage.

Prior to selling the condo to the lady who wanted to buy it, I "gifted" the property to the college. After a minute of ownership, they sold it to the new buyer. Because I didn't *sell* the property (I gave it away), my taxable gain was *zero*! The college walked away with a nice check and I avoided paying thousands of dollars in taxes. After fourteen years of ownership, I was glad to see that *someone* had finally earned some money on that condo! That started a scholarship fund that I've added to every year since making the initial gift.

Investing in Land

When the millions I'd dreamed about making on my rental properties failed to materialize, I didn't give up! In the late 1980s, my brother and I invested in 20 acres of Montana forest land. At the time many famous movie stars were buying ranches and moving to Montana, so the state was in the national spotlight. Our 20-acre property had a creek flowing through it and was adjacent to forestry land. This time, I was sure we were going to be rich!

The year after we bought the land, western Montana was besieged with forest fires. There is no better way to dissuade someone from buying land in a forest than to televise someone else's land being burnt to ashes. It took a couple of years for property values to recover to the point that our land was worth as much as we'd paid for it.

Just as property values began to increase again, the FBI found the Unabomber, Ted Kaczynski, living in a cabin nearby. A few years later, an anti-government group, called Free Men, also brought negative national attention to the area.

Add another bad year of forest fires and then, *finally* there was a growth spurt and we sold. After seven years of ownership, we were able to sell the property for $10,000 more than we'd originally paid. After subtracting real estate

6

commissions, closing costs, and seven years of interest payments, we ended up with $20,000 *less* than we'd invested!

A New Strategy

I began to realize that the problem with my investment strategy to this point was that my success depended on external market forces over which I had no control. The "buy and pray" strategy just wasn't working very well. It certainly wasn't making me rich. In fact, I was either losing money or barely breaking even. So, I decided to change my plan.

After six winters in Alaska, summers in ten other states, and a year in the Australian desert, I was tired of travel and working in remote areas. I transferred from the seismic crew into a more stable job as a computer technician working for Texas Instruments in Lewisville, Texas (a suburb of Dallas). After two years of renting an apartment there, I decided to purchase a home.

I had decided that a better way to make money in real estate was to buy fix-up properties so that I could *create* equity instead of being dependent on market appreciation, as had been the case with all of my previous investments. The country had just gone through huge banking scandals, and tens of thousands of properties had been foreclosed upon.

I found a REALTOR® who specialized in repossessed HUD homes and after making several offers, I was able to purchase a four-year-old, three-bedroom, two-bath home with a two-car garage for $60,000. After landscaping the yard and painting the house inside and out, I was living in a home that seemed just like new.

My Destiny

One weekend I went sailing with some friends on a nearby lake. My friends brought a puppy on the sailboat with them. After several hours of sailing, the dog had to pee but wouldn't go when we held him over the side of the sailboat (go figure ...). His whimpers became more frequent and he seemed pretty miserable, so we found a quiet little cove and beached the boat to allow the dog to relieve himself on shore. Somehow, I was chosen to assist the dog in this task.

While walking with the dog, I found a bleached-out real estate sign lying on the ground. The top of the sign was so sun faded that it was no longer legible, but when I flipped the sign over, there was the telephone number of a lady in Oklahoma who owned the property.

For the next few weeks I couldn't stop thinking about that lake property. There were 70 oak trees between the home site and the shoreline and four miles of open water from the beach. It was absolutely beautiful! I figured out how to drive to the property by car and would take a lawn chair and just sit there for hours, trying to figure out a way that I could own it. The lady was asking $65,000 for the land, which was $5,000 more than I'd paid for my *whole house!*

One day, while sitting in the peaceful silence of the lake, I made the decision to *go for it!* I offered the lady $50,000 cash, which she accepted. To come up with the money, I had to sell just about everything I owned (stocks, sports car, and the home I had purchased a year earlier). To show my commitment, I gave the woman a $5,000, non-refundable down payment. She gave me three months to come up with the rest of the money. I didn't know it at the time, but I'd just participated in a real estate option agreement. For three months, I had the exclusive right to buy her property, but if I didn't exercise my option within that time, she would be able to keep my down payment.

I was successful at selling all my assets, and I'm pleased to report that I *finally* made a profit on a real estate investment! In only 16 months of ownership, my investment in the HUD home earned a $19,000 profit – more than I made in 14 years from my four previous investments!

Building a Dream

I bought the lake land, drew the floor plans for my dream home on my kitchen table, and began looking for a bank to finance the construction. I thought that because I owned the land outright, it would be easy to get a construction loan. What I didn't take into account was the fact that my annual wage at the time was $32,000 and the bank used debt-to-income ratios to determine what I could afford.

After being turned down at seven banks, I was angry! My credit score was high and I'd never written a bad check in my life. Why were these banks treating me like a convicted felon? On the eighth try, I found a lender that would *partially* finance my project.

By the time my 2500-square-foot dream home was completed, I owed more than $90,000 to the bank and an additional $65,000 to family and friends. I remember driving home from the closing thinking that I'd *never* be able to repay my friends without selling the home that I'd worked so hard to make possible.

I was determined that if I could persevere through seven declined bank loans to accomplish building my dream home, I could certainly find a way to pay for it. For the next eight years, I had three roommates. Some of them stayed for two or three years, and one stayed six-and-a-half years! The rent they paid covered my mortgage, so, I was able to apply the money I'd been paying on the mortgage to repay the debt I owed to family and friends.

Within three years of building my new home, I'd earned enough money from my job, my roommates, and a printer repair business to pay off all the loans from my friends and family. I was even able to buy back the sports car I'd reluctantly sold to build the house on the lake. I was now living for <u>free</u> in my awesome lake home!

Life-changing Events

At the age of 27, my career hit a road block. I'd gotten as far as I could with my associate of science degree. Although I could still earn annual pay increases, I couldn't receive further job-grade promotions without having a bachelor's degree.

Nobody puts a ceiling on me! I went back to college and after seven years—attending classes, working full time, and building my home—I obtained a Bachelor of Science degree in business management. With my new degree, came new job opportunities. My pay increased substantially so I could easily afford the mortgage payment without roommates, but I kept them for several more years until I got married.

After being friends for ten years, Camille Trotter and I were married in 1999, just three weeks before the plant where we were employed was shut down. Raytheon had purchased our division from Texas Instruments two years earlier, and consolidated many plant sites during the reorganization process. Three weeks after our wedding, we transferred to Tucson, Arizona and began our new life together.

CHAPTER 1 - LESSONS TO LEARN FROM

Appreciation Occurs – Finally!

We sold the lake home in Texas and walked away with nearly $180,000 in equity! We bought a five-bedroom, four-bathroom home on a golf course in Tucson with unbelievable mountain views. My many winters in North Dakota and Alaska made me really appreciate the "short-sleeve" winters in Arizona.

Our home appreciated well, more than $35,000 in the first year we owned it! Due to my previous real estate experiences in North Dakota and Montana, I immediately realized the significance of this unexpected increase in value. For once, I wasn't too early or too late; my timing was perfect!

This time, I did my research and found that 2,000 people *per month* were moving to Tucson. I remember thinking, "If one house can go up $35,000 in a year, I want to own ten, or twenty!" In December 1999, we obtained an equity loan against our home for $71,000 and began investing in single-family rental homes within a one-mile radius from The University of Arizona.

We'd pay 10% down on each home and borrow the rest from banks. With our combined employment income, obtaining a loan was no longer a problem. It was actually scary what we could qualify to borrow! Because each new property created more income, the more properties we purchased, the more we were qualified to buy.

Planning for Appreciation

Purchasing a property or two each year became a habit, but we weren't relying on market appreciation to make money. Instead, we purchased properties that offered an opportunity to *create* value by adding rooms, converting garages into

11

apartments, or building a second unit on an over-sized lot. The additional square footage created instant value.

When we'd run out of money for down payments, we'd refinance a property that we'd already improved, then reinvest the proceeds in more property. Over a six-year period, the equity in our properties increased from our initial $71,000 to over *one million dollars!*

Cashing Out

By 2002, my income from real estate had surpassed the take home pay from my job, so after 22 years of a steady paycheck, I quit my job at Raytheon! I began investing in real estate full time and significantly increased my real estate earnings.

A year later, I went back to Raytheon to get Camille. I filled a limousine with friends and family (her parents came from Texas) and we picked her up from work on her 40th birthday. There was a Porsche Boxster with a big red bow waiting for her in the garage at home, but her *real* present was that she didn't have to go back to Raytheon anymore! After 20 years, she was out of the "rat race" too!

During 2004 and 2005, we sold or refinanced several properties to free up cash to purchase bigger projects. We used the proceeds to partner with other investor friends to build mobile home parks, apartment buildings, and several new homes. We expanded our market to include other Arizona cities, including Phoenix and the small town of Vail. We also started our own real estate company, Win3 Realty, and began to gain market share in Tucson. In our first year of operation, our company's sales were in the top 8% of Tucson's more than 700 real estate brokerages.

CHAPTER 1 - LESSONS TO LEARN FROM

Live Your Dreams

Quitting the job I'd held for 22 years is still the scariest thing I've ever done in my life! It took a lot of convincing to get Camille to agree to it. With the help of prayer, I gained the courage and confidence to go through with it and have never looked back. In 2005, three years after leaving Raytheon, I more than *tripled* the salary that I'd been so reluctant to leave!

I'm very fortunate to have parents who supported my ambitions and encouraged me to find ways to succeed on my own. Although my Dad passed away in 1996, my Mom is still a source of inspiration and optimism.

If I hadn't been persistent in finding a way to build the lake house in Texas, we wouldn't have been able to afford our house on the golf course in Arizona. The equity in that house gave us the down payments for the rental homes around the university, which later turned into our own "million dollar empire."

Striving to achieve one dream (the lake house) has inadvertently led me to financial freedom and a string of successful businesses. Some might say that my earliest investments were abysmal failures, but I disagree!

Finding what doesn't work helps to develop a better understanding of what does. If I hadn't experienced 14 years without appreciation in North Dakota, I wouldn't have realized the magnitude of the opportunity before me in Arizona and would never have had the courage to act on it.

Everyone has good ideas, but ideas are worthless unless you act on them. Continuing to do the same things you've always done will continue to yield the same results you've always gotten. If you never try anything new, you're *guaranteed* to repeat the past. To reap rewards, you must try new things outside your "comfort zone." This requires taking some calculated risks.

Since 2001, I've been teaching real estate investment courses at Pima Community College in Tucson, Arizona. In addition, I lecture regularly to various real estate investment groups and hold sessions at national conferences with other successful real estate investors.

These experiences have been invaluable to me because I always learn something from those I teach, and I've been able to show countless individuals how they, too, can take the steps necessary to realize their own investment goals. In addition, over the years I've been able to develop an extensive set of educational materials that I share with others.

This has formed the basis for the *Upside Up*™ series of books. The purpose of this book, *Upside Up Real Estate Investment,* is to help provide you with the knowledge, tools, and motivation you will need to be able to identify, evaluate, and acquire real estate. These things will enable you to develop the means to live your dreams

2

Why Invest
in Real Estate?

"Life consists not in holding good cards but in playing those you hold well." – *Josh Billings*

Follow the Leaders

Real estate investments can help you achieve recurring income without the daily or weekly effort required by a job. Studies have consistently shown that the wealthiest people on the planet either made their fortunes from real estate or have their money invested in real estate.

According to ResearchWorldwide.com, the world's wealthiest people have $4.9 *trillion* invested in real estate. A study conducted by the Real Estate Center at Texas A&M University found that 7.7 million high-net-worth individuals worldwide each have, on average, $640,000 personally invested in real estate, and that does not include their own homes!

The percentage of real estate ownership is highest among U.S. investors, who have an average of 29.5% of their net worth invested in real estate.

Why do the richest people in the world invest in real estate? Because of long-term appreciation, favorable income tax treatment, and a monthly cash flow that increases steadily over time as rents increase.

Benefits of Owning Income Property

Real estate investments are easy to purchase and offer the following unique combination of benefits which are unmatched by other types of investments:

1) **Leverage** - the opportunity to leverage your money, often ten to one, with inexpensive financing

2) **Growth** - the opportunity to double your money quickly through appreciation, rents, and improvements

3) **Capital Withdrawal** - the ability to refinance to recover your initial investment yet still retain ownership rights and income

4) **Controlled Appreciation** - the ability to increase the value of your investment by creating equity rather than praying that the market will drive values higher (this topic is discussed in Chapter 3)

5) **Income Tax Protection** - the ability to shield other income from taxes with depreciation allowances and deductible expenses (this topic is discussed in Chapter 4)

Leverage

When you travel to most major cities in the world, you'll notice that the tallest buildings are usually owned by banks or other financial institutions. The reason that banks are able to afford the tallest buildings in the world is because of the huge profits they make "serving" us!

The banks *pay* us interest when we deposit our money with them and they *charge* us interest when we borrow from them. The difference between what they pay and what they charge is commonly referred to as "the spread"

Usually, the difference, or *spread*, is five percentage points or more. For example, if a bank pays you 2% interest on the money in your checking account, but charges you 7% on an automobile loan, the spread is the difference of 5%.

This is a great return for the bank because the money they lend isn't even theirs! They use, or "leverage," other people's money (OPM) to create an unbelievably high profit.

As the following examples show, we can use the same method the banks use to create a higher profit for ourselves. But, this involves setting aside what many people believe to be the Great American Dream, the notion that we must strive to own our homes outright.

Using Leverage

Assume that two homes (A and B) are the same size, age, and orientation with exactly the same amenities. Each is valued at $100,000. The owners of Home A saved diligently, and were able to pay cash for their property; the owners of Home B bought their house using a 10% down payment and financed the remainder (90%) of the purchase price.

Now assume that homes in the area appreciate at the rate of 4% per year (appreciation is not something we can depend on, but we'll use it in this example to better understand the use of leverage).

If the demand for homes increases, the value of *both* homes will increase equally. The fact that Home A is paid for, and Home B is not, makes no difference to a prospective buyer. Can you imagine yourself saying, "Honey, let's get out of here! These people have a *loan!*" The amount of debt a homeowner carries has nothing to do with the property's value.

Thus, if the market value increases by 4%, both homes would increase in value by $4,000. So, the investments are equal, right? <u>WRONG!</u> The owners of Home A earned only $4,000 on a $100,000 investment (the amount of equity in the house) – for a return on investment of 4% ($4,000/$100,000 = 0.04, or 4%).

The owners of Home B *also* earned $4,000, but the owners had invested only $10,000. Home B earned a rate of return of 40% ($4,000 ÷ $10,000 = 0.4, or 40%). In other words, the owners of Home B earned *ten times more* than the owners of Home A, who paid cash for their home (see Table 2-1).

Table 2-1 Leverage Comparison #1

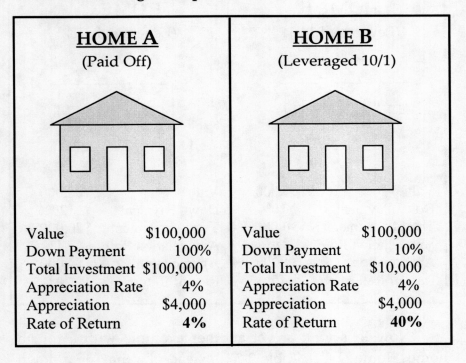

HOME A (Paid Off)		HOME B (Leveraged 10/1)	
Value	$100,000	Value	$100,000
Down Payment	100%	Down Payment	10%
Total Investment	$100,000	Total Investment	$10,000
Appreciation Rate	4%	Appreciation Rate	4%
Appreciation	$4,000	Appreciation	$4,000
Rate of Return	**4%**	Rate of Return	**40%**

Let's present another option by looking at a third home, Home C, which also is identical to Homes A and B (see Table 2-2.). Assume that Homeowner C pays a down payment of $20,000, instead of the $10,000 paid by the owners of Home B.

The property value increases by 4%, or $4,000, as it did on Homes A and B, but, the rate of return for Home C is only *half* as much as that of Home B because Homeowner C earned $4,000 on a $20,000 investment, for a return on investment of 20% ($4,000 ÷ $20,000 = 0.2, or 20%).

Table 2-2 Leverage Comparison #2

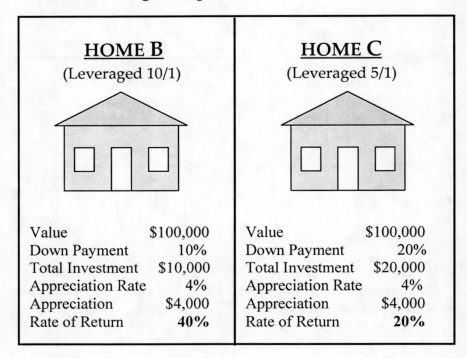

HOME B (Leveraged 10/1)		HOME C (Leveraged 5/1)	
Value	$100,000	Value	$100,000
Down Payment	10%	Down Payment	20%
Total Investment	$10,000	Total Investment	$20,000
Appreciation Rate	4%	Appreciation Rate	4%
Appreciation	$4,000	Appreciation	$4,000
Rate of Return	**40%**	Rate of Return	**20%**

Now let's look at yet another example with a fourth home, Home D (see Table 2-3). Instead of a making a down payment of 10% or 20%, assume that the owners of Home D were able to purchase the property with a down payment of only 5% ($5,000).

In this situation, the owners of Home D would realize a profit of $4,000 on a $5,000 investment for an 80% return on their investment! ($4,000 ÷ $5,000 = 0.8, or 80%).

20

Table 2-3 Leverage Comparison #3

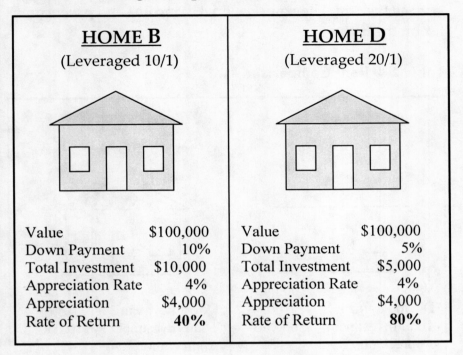

HOME B (Leveraged 10/1)		HOME D (Leveraged 20/1)	
Value	$100,000	Value	$100,000
Down Payment	10%	Down Payment	5%
Total Investment	$10,000	Total Investment	$5,000
Appreciation Rate	4%	Appreciation Rate	4%
Appreciation	$4,000	Appreciation	$4,000
Rate of Return	**40%**	Rate of Return	**80%**

The lesson to learn about leverage is that investing *twice* as much money cuts your rate of return in *half*. Conversely, investing *half* as much money *doubles* the rate of return! This is a powerful means to increase the return on your investments over a relatively short period of time.

As I explain this concept in my investment classes, many students interrupt at this point with the following argument: "The person who owns Home A paid *cash*. Because he or she doesn't have to make a mortgage payment, they get to keep all of the rent!" So I explain further.

The *cash* buyers (Homeowners A) don't actually get to keep *all* the rent. They must claim it as income and pay income tax on the money.

Table 2-4 Rent Comparison #1

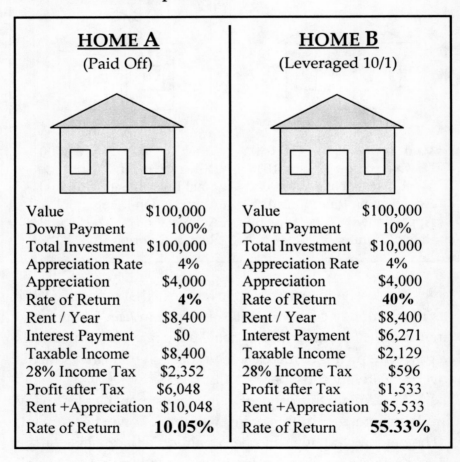

HOME A (Paid Off)		HOME B (Leveraged 10/1)	
Value	$100,000	Value	$100,000
Down Payment	100%	Down Payment	10%
Total Investment	$100,000	Total Investment	$10,000
Appreciation Rate	4%	Appreciation Rate	4%
Appreciation	$4,000	Appreciation	$4,000
Rate of Return	**4%**	Rate of Return	**40%**
Rent / Year	$8,400	Rent / Year	$8,400
Interest Payment	$0	Interest Payment	$6,271
Taxable Income	$8,400	Taxable Income	$2,129
28% Income Tax	$2,352	28% Income Tax	$596
Profit after Tax	$6,048	Profit after Tax	$1,533
Rent +Appreciation	$10,048	Rent +Appreciation	$5,533
Rate of Return	**10.05%**	Rate of Return	**55.33%**

As shown in Tables 2-4 and 2-5, there are different rates of return for purchases using different amounts of leverage after accounting for rent, mortgage interest, and income tax expenses. The *10%-down* buyers of Home B still earn more than five times as much as the *cash* buyers of Home A, and the *5%-down* buyers of Home D earn a return *10 times higher* than the *cash* buyers of Home A.

Table 2-5 Rent Comparison #2

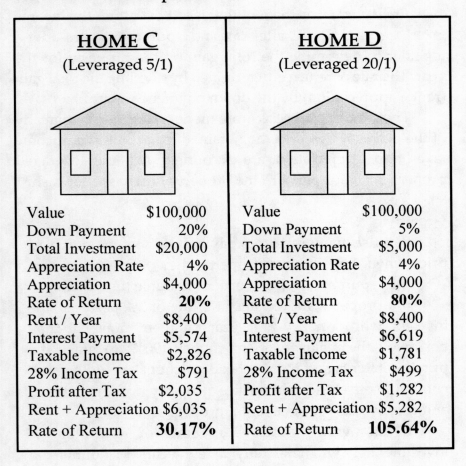

HOME C		HOME D	
(Leveraged 5/1)		(Leveraged 20/1)	
Value	$100,000	Value	$100,000
Down Payment	20%	Down Payment	5%
Total Investment	$20,000	Total Investment	$5,000
Appreciation Rate	4%	Appreciation Rate	4%
Appreciation	$4,000	Appreciation	$4,000
Rate of Return	**20%**	Rate of Return	**80%**
Rent / Year	$8,400	Rent / Year	$8,400
Interest Payment	$5,574	Interest Payment	$6,619
Taxable Income	$2,826	Taxable Income	$1,781
28% Income Tax	$791	28% Income Tax	$499
Profit after Tax	$2,035	Profit after Tax	$1,282
Rent + Appreciation	$6,035	Rent + Appreciation	$5,282
Rate of Return	**30.17%**	Rate of Return	**105.64%**

In the previous examples, the following assumptions were made: All four of the properties rent for $700 per month

($8,400 per year). The interest rate of the three financed properties is 7%. The payments differ because all three loans were for different amounts. The taxable income was calculated by subtracting the interest expense (tax deductible) from the rental income. Income tax of 28% of the taxable income was assumed for all properties.

Profit after tax is the rent that is left over after the income taxes are paid. Profit after tax and appreciation are added together to determine the total gain on the property for the year. The rate of return is determined by dividing the total gain (rent + appreciation) by the down payment amount.

The cash buyer keeps more money each month than any of the property owners who obtained loans, but after income taxes and appreciation are accounted for, the leveraged properties all out-perform the property purchased for cash.

Growth

Because many investors pay only 10% of the purchase price when they obtain a property, they only need to earn 10% of the purchase price in order to double their money.

If a property appreciates at a rate of 2% per year, the investor will earn 20% per year on their money if they borrowed the majority of the money (90%) to make the purchase. Rents and income tax deductions should be high enough to offset the debt service, property taxes, insurance, and repair costs for most rental properties.

If an investor earns a 20% rate of return on an investment, it will take only a few years to double the amount they invested. An additional profit also can be earned by charging more in monthly rent than it takes to pay the bills for the property. In addition, the amount of debt is being slightly reduced each month when the mortgage payment is made to the bank.

Profits can be driven even higher by making improvements to the property that a renter would be willing to pay additional fees to use. Examples would include adding a washer and dryer, covered parking, or storage shed. Every increase in rent creates an increase in profit, and the higher the profit, the lower the time it takes to double the investment!

Capital Withdrawal

As a property increases in value due to appreciation or added improvements, the investor owns a larger and larger share of the property. Even though the bank loaned 90% of the money required to purchase the property, *all* of the gain is yours.

When a property's value has increased 30% or more over the purchase price, my wife and I usually refinance the loan to recover some of our investment capital. This money is then invested in other properties.

To determine the value of a property, the bank hires a real estate appraiser. The appraiser evaluates market data from similar properties in the area and establishes an estimate of the property's value.

After the value has been established, we typically obtain a new loan for 80% of the appraised value and retain a 20% ownership stake in the property. The new loan we obtain is usually for a higher amount than is required to pay off the old loan, so the bank pays us the difference. This type of loan is called a *cash-out refinance*.

The check we receive from the refinance is often more than we initially invested in the property. At this point we no longer have *any* of our own money invested in the property, but we still own a 20% equity stake, receive monthly revenue from the rents, and receive income tax deductions! The money we receive from the refinance is not taxable income because refinancing is not a taxable event (selling is!).

3

Controlling Appreciation

"There is no dependence that can be sure but a dependence upon one's self." – John Gay

Market Appreciation

History has proven that appreciation occurs over time in long-term real estate investments.

As the cost of new construction continues to rise, it seems inevitable that property values will also continue to increase. While I include appreciation as a benefit, I *never* include appreciation in my calculations when purchasing property because I have no control over when and *if* it will happen.

In a free-market economy, value is driven by supply and demand. If your property is in a town that depends heavily on one employer or a military base, what would happen to property values if the plant shuts down or the base closes? When more people are leaving an area than there are moving in, an oversupply of housing occurs.

When there are more homes for sale than there are buyers to purchase them, sellers drop their prices. If one home sells at a lower price, it will have a downward affect on the value of other homes in the area.

The opposite is true in a growing area, where there is a limited supply of housing inventory. When there are more buyers seeking property than there are properties for sale, prices can increase dramatically in a very short period of time. People need a place to live and will "bid up" the price in order to obtain a home.

It's been my experience that when prices go up quickly, they either fall just as quickly or growth stagnates (sometimes for years) until the market catches up with the inflated prices. This is why I'll gladly accept appreciation when it happens but never *rely* on it in my calculations prior to purchasing a property.

CHAPTER 3 - CONTROLLING APPRECIATION

For many people, 100% of their investment strategy involves speculation that their property will appreciate. This was the basis of my initial real estate investments when I was younger, and I shared with you in Chapter 1 the abysmal results of those investments.

Controlled Appreciation

I like to use what I call, *controlled appreciation*, because it involves *creating* appreciation rather than *praying* that it will happen. Controlled appreciation doesn't depend upon outside market forces that are beyond your control.

This type of appreciation is obtained when you personally add value to the property. For example, if you build an addition onto a property, the difference between the cost to build the addition and the value of the addition is your profit. When value is added by something *you* do rather than something *the market* does, you have more control of your outcome. Improvements that add more value than they cost are solid investments.

Since investors purchase rental properties based on the rate of return the property produces, anything you can do to raise the rent will usually increase the value of a property. (I say *usually* because a hotel could earn more money renting rooms by the hour, but the property value probably won't increase because most investors don't find this type of business to be desirable.)

Here are some ways I've been able to increase rents and therefore, the property's value as an investment. By adding a washer and dryer I can usually increase the rent of my units by $25 to $50 per month because people are willing to pay more for this convenience. I've also found that I can increase rents between $50 and $75 per month by allowing pets on my properties. These two changes can create an extra $100/unit per month which would increase the property value by about $10,000 per unit. (Most real estate investors look for a rate of return of 12% or more which is 1% per month.)

I always look for "upside potential" in the properties that we purchase. By this, I mean looking for something that I can do to the property that will immediately increase the rent. When the rent is increased, the property value is also increased. Often I make income-producing changes, sometimes minor (such as the ones I just mentioned), and can generate an instant profit in a month or two. The same profit might have taken years to produce if I was relying only on rent increases or market appreciation.

Many of the changes we make are more involved, such as constructing additional rooms or units on our properties. Often these improvements create enough instant equity for us to refinance the property. As explained earlier, when we refinance our loans after creating value, we usually recover 100% *or more* of our total investment in the property. The rate of return on an investment of <u>zero</u> is *infinity!*

With other types of investments, such as stocks or CDs, the only way to get your money out is to sell the asset. When you sell a stock, the company stops sending dividend checks and when your bank account is closed, you stop receiving interest.

When a rental property is *refinanced*, you continue to collect rent, receive tax deductions, and accumulate appreciation, even though you've withdrawn all of your investment capital.

CHAPTER 3 - CONTROLLING APPRECIATION

The following pages contain the series of events that provided my wife and me with our first substantial profit using controlled appreciation.

Controlled Appreciation: An Example

In 1999, we purchased a three-bedroom, two-bath home located six blocks away from The University of Arizona, for $109,982. That may seem like a strange price, but that's the amount the property was listed for on the Multiple Listing Service (MLS). We gave the seller a full price offer, even though at the time, very few homes were selling at full price.

We probably could have negotiated a lower price, but instead we negotiated on the terms of the contract. Specifically, we asked the sellers to match our 10% down payment by giving us a seller "carry back" loan for 10% of the purchase price. At the time, most banks weren't issuing second mortgages on rental properties.

If the first mortgage is more than 80% of the appraised value, a buyer is typically required to pay mortgage insurance to protect the lender's investment. To avoid having to pay mortgage insurance, we needed to have a 20% down payment, but putting that much down would have cut our rate of return in *half*.

By paying the sellers the full price, we were able to ask them for a loan. To get a deal done, negotiations must usually offer incentives to *both* the buyer and the seller. This was a win-win deal: the sellers got the price they wanted; and, we got the financing we needed to make the numbers work for us.

Table 3-1 summarizes the various transaction details for this property.

Table 3-1 Example of Controlled Appreciation

Original Purchase	
Down Payment (10%)	$ 11,000
Bank Loan (80%)	$ 88,000
Seller Carry-back (10%)	$ 11,000
Total Cost	**$ 110,000**
Two Years Later	
Bank Loan balance	$ 86,000
Seller Carry-back balance	$ 8,000
Total Owed	$ 94,000
New Construction Loan	$ 40,000
Paid off Seller Carry-back	$ (8,000)
Paid for garage conversion	$(21,000)
Remainder of new loan (to borrower)	$ 11,000
Refinance	
New Appraised Value	$ 189,000
New Bank Loan (80%)	$ 151,200
Pay off original bank loan	$(86,000)
Pay off construction loan	$(40,000)
Cash remaining	**$ 25,200**
Expenses	
Construction loan interest (6 months)	$ (2,600)
Closing Costs (construction & final loans)	$ (5,000)
Total Expenses	**$ (7,600)**
Summary	
Cash received in excess of investment	$ 17,600
20% Equity stake in property	$ 37,800
Value created	**$ 55,400**
Positive cash flow (monthly)	$ 650

CHAPTER 3 - CONTROLLING APPRECIATION

Original Purchase

For easier math, I've rounded the purchase price for this example to $110,000. We purchased the property with a down payment of $11,000 (10% of the purchase price). We obtained a first mortgage for $88,000 (80% of the purchase price), and the seller gave us a second mortgage for $11,000 (10% of the purchase price).

The former owners of the home had used one room in the house for their ceramics hobby. They'd installed cabinets and countertops along all four walls. Immediately after closing on the property, we removed all of the cabinets, installed ceramic tile on the floor, and purchased a modular closet for this room. Having created a new, but functional, fourth bedroom, we were able to rent the home for a little more per month than the amount of our mortgage payment.

In addition to the house, there was a garage on the property. Rather than lease the garage with the house, we kept it as a central place for us to store yard tools, as well as cabinets, sinks, rental supplies, and other items we would buy on sale for use in future rental properties.

Two Years Later

After two years of receiving rent that just barely made the monthly mortgage payment, we decided to increase the income-generating potential of the property by converting the garage into a two-bedroom rental unit. We had purchased the property with the intent of exercising this option, but had been unable to find a construction lender to finance the project. We'd also been unable to find an inexpensive remodeling contractor, but in 2001, we found both and finally began construction on the garage conversion.

By this time, our original loan for $88,000 had been paid down to $86,000 and the $11,000 loan from the seller had been paid down to under $8,000, bringing our total debt to about $94,000. The private money lender that we found to finance the construction project asked how much we'd like to borrow. We calculated that we needed to borrow $40,000. The new lender wouldn't accept a third-position mortgage on the property, so we used $8,000 from the new loan to pay off the existing second mortgage being carried by the seller.

The construction cost of converting the garage to an apartment was $21,000 and the second loan payoff (to the seller) was $8,000, for a total of $29,000. Why did we borrow $11,000 more than we needed? The answer is simply that we wanted to pay ourselves! We'd spent $11,000 as our down payment to buy this property, and we wanted it back! After closing on the $40,000 construction loan, our investment in this property was *zero!*

Refinance

We now owed $86,000 on the first mortgage and $40,000 on the construction loan for a total of $126,000. When construction was complete, we planned to refinance the property with a new loan for 80% of the appraised value. The new loan would pay off both the first mortgage and the high-interest construction loan. In order to be able to pay off both loans and still have the new loan be at 80% of value, the property would have to appraise for $157,500. ($126,000 ÷ .80 = $157,500).

We were delighted when the finished project appraised at $189,000; $31,500 *more* than we'd hoped for! Instead of borrowing the $126,000 it took to pay off both loans, we obtained a loan for $151,200, 80% of the appraised value ($189,000 × .80 = $151,200). After paying off both loans, there was still $25,200 left over from the new loan! ($151,200 - $86,000 - $40,000 = $25,200). The excess money from the new loan was used to pay $2,600 for the interest on the construction loan and $5,000 for closing costs on the new loan. After paying off the loans and closing costs, there was $17,600 left over ($25,200 - $2,600 - $5,000 = $17,600). The title company issued a check to us for this amount!

Transaction Summary

At this point, we had *no money* in this property (our down payment had been repaid to us when we obtained the construction loan). The new loan was for 80% of the value, which meant we had equity in the property equal to 20% of the value, or $37,800 ($189,000 × .20 = $37,800).

In addition to the $37,800 of equity we'd acquired, we were *paid* $17,600 in cash, bringing our total profit on this project to $55,400 ($37,800 + $17,600 = $55,400). The home and newly transformed garage rented quickly. After all expenses, the property produced a positive cash flow of $650 per month!

A profit of more than $55,000 on an investment of only $11,000 creates a rate of return of more than 500%. This would be true if the money was earned in one year. Because of waiting two years before starting construction, our garage conversion wasn't completed until two and a half years after we purchased the property. Because we took so long, our *rate of return* was only 200% instead of 500% (500% ÷ 2.5 years = 200% per year).

I'm not complaining! 200% per year is still an awesome rate of return, but in hindsight, we should have started the garage construction right away. We'd purchased this property with the intention of converting the garage into a cash-producing rental unit. The upside potential was what made this property stand out above the others we'd considered.

If we'd started the construction within the first six months we owned the property, we could have completed *five* projects like this in the same amount of time!

I learned a lot from this experience. Over the past few years, we've fine-tuned this process to become extremely efficient. We've switched from remodeling garages to building brand new homes on lots zoned for duplexes. Our typical turn-around time from purchasing a property to having a new home completed is less than *three months!*

This faster pace allows us to complete *four* of these projects per year using the same investment capital, rather than *one* project every two and a half years.

Over a ten year period at our original pace, we would have completed only four projects. At our new pace, we can complete *forty* projects in the same amount of time with the same amount of money! In the future, as our properties appreciate or rents are increased, we'll receive *ten times* more because we'll own ten times more rental units.

4

Tax Savings from Real Estate

"I'm proud to pay taxes in the United States; the only thing is I could be just as proud for half the money."– Arthur Godfrey

Income Tax Protection

There are several benefits that investors receive from the government for providing housing to those who can't afford it. Before going into these incentives in detail, it's important to understand why they exist. If you understand *why* something happens, you can more accurately predict *when* it will happen and how long it will last.

The government encourages investment in housing because the housing sector provides millions of jobs; far more than most people realize. For example, when a developer decides to create a new subdivision, they employ personnel from a real estate company to locate a large parcel of land. The developer employs mortgage lenders, appraisers, surveyors, and title companies during the purchase of the land and hundreds of other people to assist in splitting the land into smaller, more affordable tracts.

Architects, draftsmen, and civil engineers spend years designing the subdivision, including the street layout, drainage, and utility services to each lot. Another survey crew is hired to locate the streets, easements, and property corners. Contractors are hired to install the underground utilities, grade the lots, and build roads. The developer pays real estate companies, banks, and title companies to sell large blocks of lots to home builders.

During the construction of the homes, hundreds of construction workers are hired including concrete finishers, framers, roofers, electricians, plumbers, drywall installers, painters, trim carpenters, and tile setters. The lumber, shingles, doors, windows, pipes, wire, air conditioners, cabinets, counter tops, floor coverings, and appliances are all purchased from manufacturing plants that employ literally thousands of other people.

As the homes are completed, the builders hire real estate sales people to advertise and sell the homes to buyers, who employ banks and title companies to complete the sale of each new home. When the homeowners get the keys, they hire movers and establish accounts with electric, gas, water, trash, telephone, and cable television companies; all of whom employ installation crews and office staff to better serve the homeowners.

Interior decorators are consulted to help select window coverings, draperies, and custom paint colors, all of which are manufactured at plants employing thousands more people. A landscaping company is employed to plant trees and bushes, lay sod, install drip-irrigation systems, and spread decorative rock. The materials for the landscaping are purchased from companies that manufacture, grow, or crush these items.

Support for all of these jobs comes from building just one subdivision in one city of the world. When you calculate the number of subdivisions in each city, the number of cities in each state, the number of states in each nation, and the number of nations in the world, the jobs created or supported by housing are enough to boggle your mind!

In addition to all of the jobs I've just listed, each company that is directly or indirectly involved in home building also employs payroll clerks, human resources personnel, accountants, attorneys and other professionals to manage the affairs of their company. It's easy to see why housing is one of the driving forces behind our economy.

Lower Your Taxes

Because housing plays such a crucial role in the nation's economy, the government encourages us to buy homes for ourselves and also to provide housing for others who can't afford a home. Those who invest in real estate are rewarded with income tax incentives, such as deductions for interest and depreciation.

Such incentives make owning a home less expensive and owning investment property more profitable. This encourages people to purchase even more real property (as opposed to personal property). For example, when you purchase a car instead of real estate, you don't receive the same favorable tax treatment. The government doesn't consider buying a car to be as desirable as buying a home, so this behavior isn't rewarded with tax incentives.

The government, however, does encourage spending money for a business-related vehicle because businesses pay taxes. Such a vehicle, presumably, will be used to help generate income for the business and, thus, the government will receive income tax revenue from the earnings. For this reason, interest paid on loans for business vehicles is a deductible expense.

When an individual buys a vehicle, the interest is not a deductible expense because the vehicle won't be used to produce revenue for the government. In addition to paying non-deductible interest on the loan, you must also pay sales tax on the purchase, licensing fees, and title transfer fees in order to use the vehicle.

There's a huge difference between having to pay taxes and receiving an income tax *refund*. Paying taxes is the consequence of not doing what the government would like us to do with our money. The government knows that if it becomes painful enough, you'll rethink the undesirable purchase and will instead invest your money in housing or businesses where they earn tax revenue.

Human behavior is controlled daily through the use of incentives and consequences. Employers offer bonuses to encourage desired behaviors and reprimands for undesired behaviors. Parents of small children use incentives and consequences as well. For example, you might tell your child, "After you clean your room, we'll go to the zoo."

This offers an incentive for your child to clean their room. Adding a consequence such as, "If you don't get your room cleaned, you can't go to the birthday party tonight," ensures that the desired task will be completed on time.

The government uses incentives and consequences with our income taxes by offering tax deductions for home ownership. If you own a home, you can deduct the cost of mortgage interest and property taxes from your gross income before calculating the income tax that you owe.

For example, let's assume that you earn $80,000 per year at your job. You pay $12,000 per year in mortgage interest and an additional $3,000 on property taxes. Table 4-1 illustrates how your taxable income will be calculated.

Table 4-1 Taxable Income after Deductions

Gross Income	$80,000
Mortgage Interest	- $12,000
Property Tax	- $3,000
Taxable Income	**$65,000**

The tax deductions for mortgage interest and property taxes come off the top of your income, which is being taxed at the highest rate you pay.

It's as if you never earned $15,000 of your pay because you're only taxed on $65,000 rather than the full $80,000 that you were really paid.

The government uses graduated tax tables which increase the tax rate as you earn more money. If you're in a 25% tax bracket and can avoid having to pay taxes on $15,000 of your income, you'll realize a tax savings of $3,750 per year ($15,000 × 28% = $3,750). That's more than $10 per day!

Quite often, an investor's income tax incentive is more than the cash proceeds from renting their property for the entire year!

Deductible Expenses

When you purchase an investment property, you effectively have started a business, and virtually *all* of your business expenses are tax deductible. The cost of mortgage interest, property taxes, hazard insurance, maintenance, repairs, improvements, vehicle mileage, and management fees may all be deductible expenses (check with your accountant).

For most investors, principal (the portion of the payment that pays down the loan) is the only expense that cannot be deducted on their taxes. Principal can't be deducted because it's money that you're actually paying to yourself.

When you write a check for the mortgage payment each month, part of the payment is for the use of the money (interest) and part of the payment goes toward paying off the amount that you borrowed (principal).

CHAPTER 4 - TAX SAVINGS FROM REAL ESTATE

Both the principal and interest *feel* like a bill because the money is subtracted from your checking account each month, but the principal portion is actually being paid to offset a debt that you owe. Paying off a portion of that debt improves your financial condition, thus is not deductible.

Keeping Records of Your Expenses

Ask your accountant for a list of the investment-related expenses that can be deducted on your income taxes. If you track expenses in the following categories, you should catch them all: advertising, automobile & travel, cleaning & maintenance, insurance, legal & professional fees, mortgage interest, other interest, repairs, supplies, property taxes, utilities, other fees & gifts, and capital improvements.

My advice is to purchase accounting software, such as QuickBooks, and hire a bookkeeper to help you set up these accounts for each property you own. This will enable you to know how each property is performing each month throughout the year. There is no need to bother your accountant with the receipts you've collected, the reports prepared by your bookkeeper should be all that your accountant needs to prepare your tax return at the end of the year.

A good bookkeeper will prepare everything in a standard format that is easy for your accountant to understand. This will save your accountant time, which means you won't be charged as much. An accountant's hourly rate is typically three to five times more than the fee a bookkeeper charges.

If instead of hiring a bookkeeper, you choose to give your accountant a shoebox full of receipts at the end of the year, you'll be charged substantially more because of the time it takes them to sort through the pile and figure out what all of the receipts are for.

During the first four months of the year, accountants are extremely busy with income tax preparation for their clients. Receipts that cannot be easily understood will probably be disregarded, which means the deduction for that item is not claimed.

The unclaimed deductions and the extra hours charged by your accountant could easily cost you more than the services of the bookkeeper for an entire year!

Why should *you* do a lot of tedious work when it actually costs less to let *someone else* do it for you?

Depreciation for Tax Purposes

Depreciation is the biggest incentive the government gives investors to own rental property. Even though most people experience *appreciation* on their property, investors are allowed to *depreciate* their rental properties by deducting a portion of the property value from their income tax each year.

To calculate depreciation, you must first separate the value of the land from the value of the improvements, or structures, on the land. The expected useful life of land is infinity, thus you cannot depreciate that portion of your investment. To determine the value of the improvements on the land, the land's value must be subtracted from your acquisition cost (the price you paid). Improvements include buildings, sidewalks, and landscaping—everything but the land. The formula to calculate the value of the improvements would be: (acquisition cost *minus* land value *equals* improvements).

44

CHAPTER 4 - TAX SAVINGS FROM REAL ESTATE

After the value of the property's improvements has been determined, that amount is divided by the time period of its useful life (the number of years you expect to be able to use the improvements on the property). This gives you the amount that can be deducted each year on your income tax return.

The U.S. government has established 27.5 years as the useful life of the improvements on a residential investment property. If you have a 30 year mortgage and are wondering how you're going to make the payments for the last 2 ½ years, don't worry! This doesn't mean that your property will implode on the day it becomes 27.5 years old.

Depreciation is simply a way to spread the purchase cost evenly over time so you can calculate your taxes. Every time a property is sold, the 27.5 year period starts over again for the new owner.

Let's assume that we purchase a property for $275,000 and that the land value is 20% of the purchase price (your accountant will establish the valuation for the land).

First, you'll need to calculate the value of the land by multiplying the purchase price by the percentage represented by the land ($275,000 × .20 = $55,000).

Next, subtract the value of the land from the purchase price to find the value of the improvements on the property ($275,000 − 55,000 = $220,000).

The remaining 80% ($220,000 in this example) becomes your basis for depreciation. You divide the value of the improvements by 27.5 years to obtain the depreciation per year ($220,000/27.5 = $8,000/yr).

To calculate your income taxes on this property, you'd first need to claim the rent you collected as income, then deduct the cost of mortgage interest, taxes, hazard insurance, and repairs, and then subtract the annual depreciation. Let's assume that the rental income is just enough to pay all of the expenses on the property each month, so there is no income. (The income was offset by expenses). The depreciation loss of $8,000 would be subtracted from other income, such as from your job or another business.

If you earn $80,000 per year, you'd subtract the depreciation loss from your income ($80,000 - $8,000 = $72,000). The depreciation from owning this one property has reduced your taxable income by 10%!

What would happen if you owned *two* properties like this? Or, better yet, *ten*? You probably wouldn't owe any taxes! (Check with your accountant because each individual has different tax circumstances, and there are limits on how much can be deducted).

5

Targeting
Your Tenants

*"The indispensable first step to getting the things you want out of life
is this: decide what you want."* – Ben Stein

Who Is Your Renter or Buyer?

After you've decided that you want to own investment property, you have to decide what type of property you'd like to own and the area in which you'd like to own it. Neither of these questions can be answered until you've first determined *who* will be renting or buying the property.

As with any new business, before you create a product, you'll need to define the customer who will purchase your product. Unless you've identified the demographic profile of your customers, you won't know whether to buy a condo, townhome, single family residence, duplex, tri-plex, four-plex, apartment building, or mobile home park.

Location, Location, Location

The area in which you buy depends heavily on the customer you're trying to attract. You'll want to buy the type of housing that each demographic group is inclined to live in. After you've matched the type of investment (duplex, single family residence, etc.) with the people you're trying to target, you'll need to determine the location that would be the most convenient for these particular types of people.

Demand is not always driven by supply. You may have the only home available in a ten-mile area, but if the home is located too far from grocery stores and other amenities, it may be hard to find a person to rent or buy this type of property for the price you need to make a profit. Be sure to consider the cost of the gasoline it would take to make the daily commute to work.

In the following sections I provide examples of what to consider when buying properties for three different demographic groups: young families, retirees, and students.

48

CHAPTER 5 - TARGETING YOUR TENANTS

Young Families

If your potential customers are young families, then you wouldn't want to buy a property without a yard. People who have children look for properties with large fenced yards and lush lawns located near highly rated schools.

It doesn't matter whether your customers are renters or buyers, school test scores are one of the most influential factors considered by people with children.

The demand for homes in an area can change overnight if the school scores change drastically in either direction. Don't buy on busy streets because traffic noise and safety will be a concern for both renters and future buyers with children.

Retirees

A home that appeals to young families may not appeal to elderly people. If the customers in your business plan are retirees (called "snowbirds" in Arizona), you'll need to offer the amenities that this age group desires. The old adage, "it's a lot easier to attract flies with honey than with vinegar" applies here.

Older people don't want to spend their golden years doing household chores like mowing the lawn. They've worked their entire lives and many have dreams of traveling in their retirement. Many people retire with a list of things that they've heard or read about during their lives, but were too busy to see while they were working.

A large house with a huge lawn and lots of maintenance is usually not a good fit for people in this stage of their life. Buy homes with easy to maintain yards that are located near a golf course. These older customers might also be attracted to a property with a small garden area and a garage/workshop.

Public transportation may be important to consider if retirees are your customer of choice. Look for two-bedroom properties close to bus routes in areas where shopping is nearby so trips to the grocery store are an easy walk or bus ride (many elderly people are unable to drive).

Close proximity to hospitals and doctor's offices is another consideration that's important to many elderly people. Health becomes a major concern later in life and can influence one's decision on where to live just as school test scores influence young parents who want the best education for their children. Check for nearby doctor's offices and also check for the availability of "meals on wheels" and other senior programs.

Students

If you plan to target students, you'll want to search for properties with multiple bedrooms near a university or community college so the student tenants can share the cost of rent with others. Properties near colleges usually sell at higher prices because of the high demand for housing in the area.

Even though most students don't have a lot of money, they don't stay home often. They usually don't have a lot of furniture, so living areas can be much smaller than usual as long as there are adequate bedroom and bathroom facilities.

If college rentals fit your business plan, but are priced beyond your budget, don't give up! Obtain a schedule of the buses or college transports that serve the student population and find a property along one of these routes. You'll be able to obtain a lower priced property farther from the campus that would still appeal to students because of the scheduled transportation to the places the students want to go.

Marketing Your Property

Before purchasing an investment property, you should consider how you plan to market the property to prospective tenants and buyers.

For example, rural properties might best be marketed at feed stores, in farm or ranch magazines, and on websites that cater to country living. Searching the classified ads in these types of publications can be helpful in determining how much rent the property might generate or what the average sale price is for the area. These ads can also tell you how competitive the market is for that type of property.

Upside Up™ in Real Life

College Newspapers

If you're marketing to students, to get extra value for your money, find out if the college newspaper suspends publication during the summer months or semester breaks (times when vacancies also occur). If the paper suspends service during these times, find out when the last newspaper will be published (in print and online) and run your ad on that day.

By paying to advertise for only *one day*, your ad will remain on the school newspaper's website for *free* during the three months over the summer and the few weeks between semester breaks. Using this virtually unknown tactic, I've found many tenants, even for homes I purchased *after* placing the ad.

College properties are best served with advertisements in the student newspaper, not only because this is what the students read, but also because these ads are usually much cheaper than the local newspaper. Most college students are computer literate and many are ecologically sensitive, thus prefer to read the paper online. Be sure to pay the extra few dollars to place your ad on the newspaper's website in order to reach the largest audience.

If retirees are your target market, then homes on or near a golf course might be the properties you target for investment, and golf magazines might be the best advertising channel to reach your audience.

Finding Your Niche

A niche can best be described as a "hole" in the products or services offered by your competition. When you know your customers well enough to understand their needs, you'll begin to find features and amenities that they desire but your competition doesn't offer.

Providing these desired amenities to consumers can give you an advantage over your competition. Creativity and imagination can help to develop a product that is specifically tailored to the customers in your target market.

To compete in a niche market, you'll need to collect data on your targeted group and compile a profile based on demographics, such as age and gender to establish who they are, where they live, what they do in their spare time, how much they earn, what they buy, and why they need your product or service.

Start developing your niche by finding out what perks your competitors offer to your target market. Use the information you compile to devise incentives and added features that your competition doesn't offer.

When you offer amenities that your competition doesn't, *your* property becomes more desirable to the customer than your competitor's. This added desirability is your competitive advantage over other properties and the reason that customers will be compelled to choose you over your competitor.

Your niche should align with your mission statement and what you hope to become known for providing in the marketplace. Before introducing a new idea, pre-test it on potential customers to find out if the idea is feasible.

Upside Up™ in Real Life

Furnished Units

My wife and I purchased a property in 2000 that had a small apartment attached to the rear of the main home. A co-worker expressed a desire to rent the small unit if it were furnished. He traveled to Tucson for five to eight days per month on business yet had no desire to move permanently since he and his family resided in another state.

To accommodate his request – and to secure him as a tenant – my wife and I went furniture shopping. We were able to buy enough new or relatively new furniture (from garage sales and newspaper ads) to fill the entire one-bedroom apartment for less than $200!

We added $50 per month to the advertised rental price to compensate for the furnishings. After four months, our investment was repaid by the higher rent.

Our original tenant is still renting the small apartment after nearly *eight years!* Over that time period, our initial $200 investment for furniture has yielded an additional $4,800 in rental income for a cumulative return of 2400%!

Some examples of niche marketing include: converting apartments into condos to create affordable home ownership, buying exercise equipment and converting a studio apartment into a weight room for health-conscious tenants, and renting fully-furnished apartments across the street from hospitals for traveling medical personnel.

If low price is your niche, you can lure price-sensitive customers by offering move-in specials like one-half month free with a one-year lease, discounts for on-time rent payments or good grades, rent guarantees for lease renewals, referral payments for those who bring in new tenants (check with your attorney to ensure this is legal), and appreciation gifts like restaurant certificates at Christmas and after lease renewals.

Unit Mix

Whether you've decided to purchase a duplex or a multiplex with several units, you'll want to consider unit mix (the number of studio units, one-bedroom units, two -bedroom units, and so on).

Unit mix is important because it's a way to measure how much time it will take to manage the property in relation to how much money it brings in. No matter how large or small a unit is, it requires a lease, and each lease requires a fixed amount of time and money to maintain.

Larger units typically require less time, money, and risk to manage than do smaller units. Keep that in mind when you begin shopping for rental properties.

During vacancies, you'll need to advertise the property for rent. The newspaper charges the same rate to advertise a studio apartment as it does for a four-bedroom home. If the ad costs $100 for a weekend, and the studio apartment rents for

$300, one weekend of advertising represents one-third of a month's rent! If your vacant unit is a four-bedroom that rents for $1,200, then the $100 ad represents only one-twelfth (about 8%) of the monthly rent.

When you invest in a rental property, you'll want to know how long it will take to recover your money. At four times the rent, the four-bedroom unit will repay your investment much faster than the studio unit and it will take less time to manage. (The cost to buy a four-bedroom unit will be more than the studio, but typically not four times as much).

You'll have to show the property to perspective tenants, go over the lease with them, verify their credit, and then stay in communication with them each month after it's rented. Would you rather receive $300 per month for your time or $1,200?

Turnover also enters into the equation. A studio apartment is the *entry level* of rental properties. There are no bedrooms in this type of unit, so the tenants must sleep in the living area. The only room with a closeable door is the bathroom.

Many people who rent these entry-level units either make it on their own and move up to a one-bedroom unit, or they fail and move back home with their parents or wind up back on the street. Either way, they *leave*, which means you'll have to clean the unit and pay to advertise it again.

This can happen several times in a year. Between the lost rent during vacancies, and the cost of advertising, cleaning, and re-renting the unit, it may actually cost you more money to manage the unit than you collect in rent!

Another factor to consider is the security deposit, which is usually based on a percentage of the monthly rent. In the

Tucson rental market, for example, one month's rent is typically the amount of the security deposit. In the previous example, with rents of $300 for the studio unit and $1,200 for the four-bedroom unit, you would be able to collect a $300 deposit for the studio unit and $1,200 for the four-bedroom unit.

Which tenant has the most to lose for damaging your property? Would you rather have $300 of their money or $1,200? If the tenant were to accidentally break something in the studio, they'd know that their small deposit would need to cover the broken item. With most or all of their security deposit thus obligated, how clean do you think they'll leave the unit if they're not likely to receive any money back?

The tenants in the four-bedroom unit represent a much lower risk to me. Because they have four times more money at stake, they're more likely to take care of the property than people who have very little to lose if they destroy the property.

People who rent four-bedroom units are usually more entrenched than those who rent studio units. They have a propensity to stay longer because they either have children in school or multiple roommates who would all have to agree to move. In addition, they'll probably have a lot more personal belongings than someone in a studio apartment, making it much more cumbersome to move.

When the tenants stay longer, there's less wear and tear on the property from banging into doors and walls while moving furniture. You spend less money on cleaning and advertising, and less of your time showing vacant units. I tell my customers that if they're considering owning a 30-plex with all studio units, they might as well move into the property because they're going to be there all the time anyway!

There are always exceptions to any generalization. Studio units could provide a reliable source of income (and a huge profit) near a college campus or in downtown areas of major cities.

Many executives live in remote suburbs and work long hours in high-rise office buildings. On occasion, it may make sense for these professionals to stay near their office during the work week rather than fight traffic for several hours in each direction of their commute.

These rental units could be shared by several executives who would be willing to pay much higher rent than a full-time tenant would be inclined to pay. A studio unit would provide a place to shower and catch a few hours of sleep between their grueling workdays.

Combining Small Units

You could think "out of the box" and consider ways to combine several of the smaller units to make them easier to manage. For example, two studio units might be converted to one two-bedroom/two-bath unit by using the extra kitchen as a laundry room, and converting the extra living area into two bedrooms.

By doing this, your unit count decreases, making it half as expensive to manage and less time consuming to maintain and show. Because the length of each tenant's stay is typically longer in a two-bedroom unit than in a studio, the combined unit is less expensive to advertise. You'll have less wear and tear from people moving in and out, and fewer cleaning bills between leases. What a difference this change could make to your profit margin!

This concept makes a lot of sense on five-unit properties. Lenders can't sell loans on the secondary market if there are more than four units on the property. These types of loans must be held by the issuing bank, which limits their flexibility and reduces their profit. Because these loans cost *them* more, banks charge *you* more.

Upside Up™ in Real Life

<u>Combining Units</u>

In 2007, we purchased a duplex that was situated at the back of a huge lot. The property had plenty of room to build a new home at the front of the property, but, per zoning regulations, it did not have enough land area to qualify for *three* units.

We came up with a plan to reconfigure the duplex into a single-family home. This would allow us to build a new home at the front of the lot without exceeding the two-unit limit imposed by the zoning regulations.

During the renovation process, we discovered that, in fact, the property had *originally been* a single-family home! We returned the home to its original configuration by removing the walled-in doorways. The kitchen sink and stove in one unit were replaced with a washer and dryer. A wall with a door was added in one of the living rooms to create a third bedroom.

By combining the two small duplex units into one single-family home, we were able to build a new home at the front of the lot and create a profit of $40,000.

Combining two of the units on a property such as this would change it into a four-unit property, which would allow the loan to be sold on the secondary market. Because of this change, the interest rate on the loan might decrease by as much as two percentage points because the issuing bank would no longer have to retain the loan in its portfolio.

A potential downside of converting the units is that the rent for a two-bedroom may not be as much as two rents for the studios. The difference in rent might be offset by the high vacancy rate of the studios due to constant turnover. When all costs are considered, the studio vacancy could easily cost more than the difference in rent between one two-bedroom unit and the two original studio units.

Another thing to consider is whether or not all the units are on one "master" meter. If each unit is separately metered, the electric services would have to be combined so the new combined unit would receive only one electricity bill.

A Fish Story

If you put all of this information into a fishing analogy, it makes a lot of sense. Wake up early in the morning because that's when the fish bite (timing is everything). The first thing you'll need to decide is *where* you want to fish (location to invest). The bodies of water you choose to fish in is determined by what *types* of fish (buyers/tenants) are known to have been caught there in the past.

Once you've chosen the location of *where* to fish, you'll need to decide which bait to use to attract the fish (advertising). Whether you use worms or grasshoppers, jigs or lures is determined by the type of fish (social demographic) that you want to catch.

You'll know whether to rent a boat, or use waders, by talking with the people at the bait shop (investment clubs) who have conversations with other fishermen all day long. These are the people with their thumb on the pulse of fishing in the area—so be sure to listen to what they have to say.

The moral of this fish story is simple; know what your customers want and give it to them. It's human nature to take the path of least resistance. If your property is located in an area frequented by the potential buyers/tenants, has the amenities this specific group is known to desire, and is advertised in places they'll notice, you'll be successful with your investment.

If you go out and buy the first property you find without creating a business plan (like I did in 1982), you may get lucky every once in a while, but over time, you're going to lose more times than you win.

6

Creating Your Strategy

"Nothing happens by itself... it all will come your way, once you understand that you have to make it come your way, by your own exertions." – Ben Stein

Know Who to Buy For

The fact that you made it this far in the book indicates that you were intrigued enough by the many benefits of owning investment property that you decided to learn what kind of properties to look for.

If you've jumped ahead to start looking at property before you've read the previous chapters, I suggest that you go back and read from the beginning. The first thing you must do in any business is define your customers. I explained this earlier, but if you skipped over it, I'll explain it again in more detail. It's worth repeating anyway.

If you don't know *who* will rent or buy your properties, you won't know what type of properties to buy or where to buy them. You must define your customer *before* you buy to ensure that there's adequate demand for your property.

The amenities desired by college students are much different from those of retirees, and different still from families with children. Let's say that you purchase a vacant lot in an area where many retirees are buying second homes. If you construct a large three-story home, you'll probably encounter a problem because you've overbuilt the area and haven't matched your product to the needs of your customer.

If you'd researched other homes in this area, you would have probably found that most retired people who buy a second home usually purchase a smaller home rather than a larger one.

Many of these "empty nesters" no longer have the need for several bedrooms because their children are grown and gone. Because many older people have difficulty climbing stairs, or worry about falling, the three-story home that you built will probably not appeal to many in your target audience unless you install an elevator.

When your property doesn't sell, you might try to rent it, as many investors do. The problem is that retirees who rent don't want to climb the steps either! Whether you're renting or selling, you'll be forced to lower your asking price until you find someone who's willing to deal with the size of the home and all of those stairs.

Now, let's assume that you did your research before you started and built a different home on the same lot. Because you knew in advance that the area appeals to elderly people, you constructed a single-story home with low-care landscaping on a drip-irrigation system. The landscaping would require very little maintenance and would continue to prosper during long absences by the owners.

Your bathrooms would have garden tubs for those who like to soak in the tub to relax. They'd also have walk-in showers with grab bars to accommodate people with physical limitations such as bad knees or hip replacements. The bathrooms and doorways would be extra-wide so those using walkers or wheel chairs could maneuver easily.

The garage would be extra wide to accommodate a workshop area with plenty of shelving for the hobbies and crafts that occupy the time once spent at work.

If you were a retiree, which home would you choose? The choice would be obvious because your home was built to meet the needs of your customer. Demand for this home could cause a bidding war at the same time the owners of the large three-story home would be lowering their price!

Wouldn't it be nice to know *before* you buy a home that nobody will be willing to rent it at the amount you would need to make your mortgage payments? When you've identified all of your customers' needs, you can create a desirable product that satisfies their needs and yours.

People will pay more to get what they want, but have no motivation to rent or buy what doesn't suit them. For this reason, much of your planning must be completed *before* you begin searching for property.

Flip or Hold?

Before you purchase an investment property, consider how long you intend to own the property. If you plan to keep the property as a long-term investment, you'll want to find a neighborhood where properties appreciate faster than average and ongoing fees, such as association dues, are low.

If you plan to make improvements on the property and sell it right away (this is known as a *flip*), then you'd want to limit your search to neighborhoods where few houses are for sale and the average days required to sell a home is very low.

You won't want the profit created by your improvements to be eaten up by mortgage payments while you're waiting for it to sell. This problem affects many investors who don't plan well, and can quickly turn their flip into a *flop*!

Buy Low, Sell High

"Buy low, sell high" is an old adage that sounds more like common sense than advice. People who successfully flip houses will tell you that they make their money on the purchase, not on the sale. If the profit numbers are low for a project, negotiate hard.

In your business plan, along with your other assumptions, you should have a *written* profit minimum that you're willing to accept on each type of investment project. The minimum should take into account the amount of risk that's involved and the amount of time the project will take to complete.

Be sure to leave room in your assumptions for some unexpected circumstances, but not so much that the extra "fluff" makes it impossible to find a deal. Remember, you don't earn any money unless you actually *buy* something!

Properties that are priced very low are going to attract offers in any market. Because of the heightened competition for low-priced properties, negotiating even a little may cause you to lose a deal.

Upside Up™ in Real Life

Get the Deal!

In 2002, long before the crazy seller's market began in Tucson, my wife and I paid $150,000 for a home that was listed for $139,900. People around us thought we were crazy at the time, but this house was under-priced and we knew there would be a lot of interest from other buyers.

In the first twenty-four hours after the home went on the market, the seller received five offers to purchase the property. Our offer was accepted because it was higher than the others and set the closing date at ten days after contract acceptance. I found out later that we'd only beat the next highest offer by $2,500.

We built on the property and sold it two years later for a profit of $125,000! If we hadn't made the "crazy" offer, we never would have gotten the deal.

There's always someone else who's willing to earn a lower profit than you. If your business plan shows a profit higher than your minimum, it doesn't matter what the asking price is; pay what you need to pay to get the deal!

Many novice investors think they must buy below the asking price in order to get a good *deal*. It's hard to rationalize, but you have to stop thinking about the purchase price; it's not important. What matters is whether or not you can earn a profit greater than the minimum you've written in your business plan.

Don't let your ego get in the way of your profits. We're surrounded by people who have great ideas but fail to act on them. That's exactly why a good investor creates a business plan with their criteria *in writing*.

When the fears start to take hold, go back to your written investment plan and follow it! Get your plan in writing *before* the emotion of a property purchase enters into the equation.

Value, Motivation, and Upside

There are three things to look for when purchasing a property: value, seller's motivation, and upside potential.

Value - means that the property is better than average when compared to similar properties that are for sale.

Value may come from a lower price per square foot, higher rents, lower expenses, or perhaps favorable financing, such as an assumable loan at an interest rate that is lower than the rate currently available on the market.

To locate undervalued properties, you could have your REALTOR® search a specific neighborhood for properties that are listed below a certain price per square foot, below a specific gross rent multiplier (GRM), or above a minimum capitalization rate.

Also search for properties that have assumable bank financing or owner financing. More information is provided on these topics in Chapter 12.

Motivation - A seller's motivation varies depending upon his or her situation. There are several circumstances that create a *must-sell* situation for sellers. When distress sales can be found, they usually represent a great opportunity for buyers to get a good deal. When people *need* to sell fast, the prices are usually well below market value. Finding these deals is often the hardest part of investing. Several potential places to look and what to look for are provided as follows.

Foreclosures: Some sellers are in a must-sell situation because they're facing foreclosure. The clock is ticking and it's only a matter of time before they'll lose their home and destroy their credit.

Sellers in the early stages of foreclosure (called pre-foreclosure) are usually the most willing to negotiate. These people have gotten into financial trouble and don't have many options to get out from under the burden of their debts.

Finding out about foreclosure and pre-foreclosure properties can sometimes be difficult. Though searches of foreclosure databases or public records published in newspapers can yield some leads, the best deals are often snapped up quickly by others. A better strategy is to contact real estate agents who have privileged or exclusive access to information about these deals.

Properties on the market a long time: Sellers whose properties have been for sale a long time, but haven't sold, may not be desperate, but they're probably worried about selling their home. Your REALTOR® can search for properties based on the number of days they've been on the market. Also look for property listings that have recently expired, were withdrawn from the MLS database, or on which the price was recently reduced.

Upside Up™ *in Real Life*

<u>Long Time on Market</u>

In 2005, we found a multi-unit property that had been for sale for more than a year. The previous owner had not maintained the property well and it was in a terrible state of repair. The units were poorly equipped and downright *nasty!*

One of our clients has an appetite for this type of property. In making his purchase offer, he negotiated so well that the seller, who seemed really desperate to unload the property, had to bring more than $30,000 to the closing in order to pay off his loan!

Our client totally renovated the three existing units, removed an antiquated mobile home from the adjacent lot, and built two new, free-standing rental homes in its place. After constructing the new homes, he refinanced his loans and recovered *all* of his investment capital (to use on other projects). He and his wife now collect more than $3,000 per month in rent, which is a nearly $800 *more* than their bills!

Bank-owned properties: Banks refer to these properties as *real estate owned* properties (or *REOs*). Lenders don't like to own real estate because they can't earn interest and origination fees from loans when their money is tied up in repossessed homes.

They may be willing to discount the price they're asking if you can close quickly and return their money to them so they can get it working again. Obtaining your loan from the lender who repossessed the property will strengthen your offer because you're enabling them to earn a profit from the new loan while absorbing a loss on the previous loan. Your real estate agent can help you search for lender-owned properties.

Corporate-owned properties: Corporations sometimes purchase properties from their employees when they relocate them from one area to another. They, like banks, don't care to own the properties, so they may be willing to negotiate a lower price if they could get their money back sooner.

Employees who have relocated and didn't have the option of selling their home to their employer might be able to sustain two mortgage payments for a few months, but usually, after a few months of double payments, they begin to reduce their price.

Builder inventory: Home builders *hate* to carry inventory. They pay 12% or more in annual interest which is charged by the month. If a home doesn't sell shortly after it is completed, the builder could easily lose their entire profit on the project to debt service (also known as carrying costs).

When demand is high, home builders have lotteries to decide which buyers will win the right to buy their homes. When the tables turn and there are more homes than there are people willing to buy them, the home builders give a tremendous number of incentives, including thousands of dollars in free upgrades, closing-cost credits, several months of free payments, and higher commissions and bonuses to real estate agents for selling the homes. Use this knowledge to negotiate when the market is slow.

Upside Up™ in Real Life

<u>Builder Inventory</u>

Some clients of ours found a newly-constructed home that, while completed more than a year earlier, had not been sold. Using this to their advantage, the couple was able to negotiate the purchase of the property for 20% less than the initially advertised price, a savings of more than $80,000.

Builders are not in the business to *hold* houses. They need to sell them as soon as they're completed. The largest profit for a builder is the markup on upgrades (such as kitchen cabinets, bathroom fixtures, flooring, and options). When you purchase a home that is already built, many times, the builders will sell it at or below cost just to recover their investment capital so they can build more homes.

For our clients, not being able to choose their colors turned out to be worth $80,000!

Upside - Upside can be best described as value that you *create*. No matter what type of property you decide to purchase, your business plan should provide a means of creating value. This takes the guesswork out of investing. Most people buy real estate and wait for it to increase in value.

This "buy-and-pray" method can prove to be an emotional roller coaster because markets go up and down due to reasons beyond your control. If you happened to buy at a high point and the market swings to a low point when you need to sell, you'll lose a significant amount of money.

CHAPTER 6 - CREATING YOUR STRATEGY

If your plan includes *creating* value and you invest the same amount steadily through the highs and lows, you'll do well even in the down markets and will have money to invest another day. Value is created when you *do* something to make the price increase. Profit can be realized in any market if you make a change that causes the value to increase more than the cost of the change.

I've made far more money from improving properties than I've ever made from finding under-priced properties from motivated sellers. Creating value involves looking past the way a property is currently configured to determine the highest and best use possible.

Upside Up™ *in Real Life*

Add Square Footage

My business partners and I found a three-bedroom, two-bath home that had a detached two-car garage. We converted the garage into a two-bedroom guest house and built a two-bedroom, one-bath addition onto the main house.

Our target market for this home was an adult care provider. Instead, we ended up renting the property to a four-generation family. The youngest generation is in grade school and the great-grandparents are in their eighties, so these people are likely to be very long-term tenants.

They've been living at this property for more than three years, and were a huge selling point to the new buyer when we divested the property in 2004.

For example, if a two-bedroom, one-bath home on a busy street near a university has commercial zoning, the highest and best use of the property is not renting to college students. You could probably get a lot more rent if you configured it as an office and rented it to professionals, such as attorneys, accountants, or insurance agents.

Converting the kitchen into a break area/copier room, the bedrooms into offices, and the living room into a conference room would transform the property from a residential rental to a commercial office building. Depending upon your area, the commercial rent would probably be at least two or three times as much as the residential rent for the two-bedroom home. In addition, the professionals who rent the property would be less likely to have late-night parties than student tenants.

Upside Up™ in Real Life

Add a Guest House

My friends built a new two-bedroom house in their back yard. The house has a separate entry off the driveway, and with a separating wall and locking gate, can easily be isolated from their home.

They currently use the building as their home office, but a future buyer might use the house as a rental unit to offset a portion of their mortgage payment. Other buyers might find it perfect for their aging parents.

Due to advances in medical science and a better awareness of health, people are living much longer. Properties such as this that can easily be adapted to fill different needs will appeal to many people and thus will be in high demand.

The ability to *see* what isn't there can be developed over time. First you must understand the needs of the marketplace.

If you know that there is a strong desire for certain amenities and you provide them, you'll be successful.

When you look for ways to create more value than currently exists, you gain control of your profit. The most common method real estate investors have found to create value is buying fix-up homes. These homes are sold at lower than average prices because they need work. When the properties are rehabilitated, they may sell for higher than average prices depending on how well the rehabilitation work was done.

Upside Up™ in Real Life

__Laundry Facilities__

We install washers and dryers in all of our rental properties because people will pay more each month to avoid the hassle of hauling their clothes to the Laundromat and watching them spin for hours each week. Because our properties satisfy a need, they tend to rent faster and for more money than those that don't satisfy the needs of the tenants.

Slapping paint and slobbering caulking over defects is not the way to make a profit. Unfortunately, this is the approach that many investors take when "fixing" a house. The shoddy workmanship can be spotted a mile away.

If a potential buyer finds one area of the house where shortcuts were taken, they begin to wonder what else might be covered up in other areas. Unless the market selection is extremely limited, this concern will cause the buyers to purchase another home with better workmanship.

Any rehabber can make a lot of money by fixing and flipping homes when the market is hot. During these times, buyers have few choices and are forced to purchase homes with poor workmanship and cheap fixtures. When the market is slow, rehabbers will fail to produce the same results unless they improve the quality of their repairs.

Other opportunities to create value involve adding square footage to a property. Older homes often don't have large enough bedrooms or an adequate number of bathrooms to meet the needs and desires of today's families.

Building a master suite onto the home can transform a three-bedroom, one-bath home that wouldn't sell, into a four-bedroom, two-bath home with a bidding war. Giving the market what it wants can produce amazing results!

To find opportunities for building, look for homes on large lots, small homes with only one bathroom, and properties that are under-built for their zoning.

If you really want to think out-of-the-box, look for older mobile homes in desirable neighborhoods. You can either replace the old mobile home with a newer manufactured home or remove the mobile home and construct a site-built home on the property.

Either way, you'll need to do your research to determine the value of other manufactured homes or site-built homes in the area. Pay close attention to how much they've sold for and how long it took for them to sell

7

Properties
to Consider

"Choice has always been a privilege of those who could afford to pay for it." – Ellen Frankfort

There are several different types of real estate to consider before investing. In this chapter, many of the pros and cons are provided for the following investment types:

- Single Family Residences
- Duplexes
- Tri-plexes and Four-plexes
- Mobile Homes
- Condos and Townhomes
- Apartment Complexes
- Land

Single Family Residences

Single-family residences (SFRs) are easy to find and easy to finance. The most obvious downfall of buying SFRs for rentals is that all of your eggs are in the same basket. If your tenants move out and your unit is vacant for a month or two, *all* of your rental income is gone.

On the positive side of the equation, I've found that single-family homes are much easier to rent because they have a private yard and no shared walls with neighboring tenants. Because the utilities are not shared with other tenants, all the bills are typically paid by the tenant, which reduces month to month fluctuations in your profit by wasteful tenants.

In my experience, SFRs appreciate faster than other types of rental property because they appeal to more people.

Value is often driven by external market forces, but demand for single family homes is usually much higher than demand for multiplex units which appeal only to investors.

When it's time to sell, as in most businesses, the more people your product appeals to, the higher the demand will be. High demand usually brings high price, depending on supply.

Single-family residences can easily go from being a rental property to an owner-occupied home without structural changes. This is the only property type that has this chameleon-like quality. If the market has gone too soft to sell your property, you simply rent it until the conditions are favorable to sell.

Duplexes

I define a duplex as two units on one lot, not necessarily connected to one another. Duplexes can be a great way to obtain home ownership for those who are just starting out.

This type of investment offers the best of both worlds because you apply some of the money you once spent on rent to equity and you have someone else helping you pay all the expenses that come with home ownership. For single people, the option exists to further your gain by sharing your portion of the property with a roommate or two. After taxes, it's quite possible to live for free in this type of arrangement.

Let's assume that the monthly mortgage payment on your duplex is $1,200 and that the tenants in the rented unit pay $700 in rent. This leaves $500 to be paid by the owner-occupied unit.

If you find a roommate to share your unit, that person would probably pay $350 plus half of all utilities. (This is the market rent indicated by the unit rented next door)

You now have $1,050 of the $1,200 payment being paid by other people. The tax advantages of owning the property are all credited to *you*, even though your roommate and the other tenants are paying 87.5% of the payment for you. If the property appreciates in value, *all* of the appreciation belongs to you even though 90% or more of the money to buy the property came from a bank.

I haven't found any other investment that is as lucrative for potential profit. When the occasional repair is necessary, half of the expense is tax deductible (Check with your accountant - you can't deduct expenses on the unit you live in).

Upside Up™ *in Real Life*

<u>See What Isn't There</u>

Some of our clients purchased a duplex that consisted of a one-bedroom unit and a two-bedroom unit. The one-bedroom unit had a large laundry room. My clients moved the washer and dryer into an outside storage shed and converted the laundry room into a second bedroom.

The two-bedroom unit had an enclosed porch that they converted to a third bedroom. Because of their alterations to the property, they were able to collect an additional *six hundred dollars* per month in rent. The total cost of the alterations was repaid by the higher rent in less than two years.

Financing costs for a duplex are usually about the same as those of a single-family home. If you later decide to move and rent both sides to tenants, then *all* expenses become tax deductible.

A duplex offers better financial security than a single family home because if one unit becomes vacant, only half of your income stream is affected. Duplexes are usually easy to resell because they're the property type most sought after by mom-and-pop investors who are just starting out in real estate investing.

Tri-plexes and Four-plexes

The more units you own, the more independent sources of income you have. With four or more units, for example, you should be able to have one unit empty and still be able to make your mortgage payment from the remaining rents. This is a nice safety net, but it comes with consequences.

As you increase the number of units you own, you'll also increase the time and money required to maintain those units. Instead of owning a home with one water heater, one furnace, one air conditioner, one stove, one refrigerator, and one dishwasher, you now own several of each that will need to maintained, repaired, and replaced over time.

The more units you own, the more time you'll spend maintaining the *relationships* with the tenants. Besides communicating with the tenants periodically, each rental unit requires advertising, showing, preparing a lease, conducting the initial walk-through inspection, monthly rent collection, scheduling occasional repairs, meeting housekeepers and carpet cleaners, and conducting a move out inspection.

As one tenant vacates, a new tenant arrives and the cycle starts all over again. Many people begin using a property management company when they get too many units to manage themselves, but this cuts into your profits.

The interest rate charged by a lender on a tri-plex is typically higher than that of a single-family home or a duplex, and interest rate on a four-plex is higher still. As the number of units increase, lenders assume more risk because fewer people are able to afford them.

Lenders are concerned that a smaller market of buyers will make these properties harder to sell if they have to foreclose. They charge more up-front fees and a higher interest rate to cover their *potential* for loss, even if it never happens.

Properties with more than four units cannot be sold on the Fannie Mae or Freddie Mac secondary markets, so the bank must keep the loan in their portfolio of investments. Banks usually charge a premium on these *portfolio loans* because they're committing the money for a very long time.

Many lending institutions are unwilling to lend their money for long terms because they lose the ability to leverage their money.

Mobile Homes

There's definitely a right way and a wrong way to own and maintain "wheel estate," (also known as manufactured homes). These types of investments are usually much less expensive to buy than site-built structures. Because the cost to purchase a manufactured home is lower, the rent for the unit is lower as well.

When the price of site-built homes surpasses the amount that people can afford to pay, manufactured homes are a good alternative to fill the gap. Although building standards for these homes have improved dramatically since the 1970s, the maintenance costs are still extremely high due to the use of non-conventional piping, sinks, drains, and electrical wire.

Most major home improvement stores don't carry supplies for manufactured homes. These parts typically need to be purchased from specialty stores that stock replacement parts for manufactured homes.

Due to the limited availability of these types of stores, the prices of the parts they carry are often substantially more expensive than similar products available at The Home Depot, Lowe's, or other home improvement stores.

For example, a ten-gallon water heater for a one-bedroom manufactured home can easily cost more than the 40-gallon water heater that is common in most site-built homes.

One of the reasons the mobile home business is so lucrative is because of the social stigma attached to mobile homes. The manufactured-housing industry has been trying to shake the "trailer" label for over 30 years but it still is prevalent in the minds of investors and the general public. The term "trailer trash" is another stigma to overcome. The tenants that you'll attract to occupy your manufactured homes correlate directly to the age and condition of your property.

If you have nice, clean units in a safe neighborhood, you'll be able to charge more rent and attract good, honest people. If you provide dirty, run-down units in a scary neighborhood, you'll probably rent them, but the people you'll attract will be desperate. Your turnover rate on these units will be high and you'll be on a first name basis with local judges due to continuous eviction proceedings. You can't plant wheat and expect corn to come up; you reap what you sow.

Mobile homes are hard to finance, so you may need to pay cash to purchase the units. The rents or lease purchase payments you'll receive compared to the amount of money you initially invest make these investments some of the biggest "cash cows" in real estate. When it's time to sell, you'll need to find other investors who've overcome the social stigma of owning manufactured housing.

Upside Up™ in Real Life

<u>Wheel-Estate Management</u>

In 2005, we purchased a run-down mobile home park that was by far the worst *eyesore* in the neighborhood. To clean up the park, we offered to give these older units to the tenants if they would, at their expense, move the units to another mobile home park down the street. Within a few months, we'd cleared the property.

We moved newer manufactured homes onto the property and *sold* them to the new occupants on the day they moved in. Because the tenants *own* the unit, they also own the maintenance for the unit. Thus our cost of repairs is *zero!*

We sold the units on a seven-year *contract for deed*, which means that we carry the loan and the buyers pay us back in installments over a seven-year period. Because we've made it easy for our customers to obtain ownership with a low down payment and seller financing, we can sell these homes for twice the amount we paid to purchase them.

The down payment is usually enough to recover the cost of moving the home and setting it up on our property. The buyer's payments are set up so that all of the money we've spent to purchase the home would be recovered after three years. The remaining four years of the contract become a period of *pure profits!*

Where once there was an eyesore, we now have newer homes with solid tenants who pay their own utility bills, send the lot rent and loan payment on time, and *never* call with any maintenance issues.

CHAPTER 7 - PROPERTIES TO CONSIDER

I would not recommend buying units much more than ten years old since you'll be competing against the mobile home dealerships for clientele. These dealerships make it extremely easy to purchase a brand new home with the land all wrapped into one loan. They provide a set up service and connect all of the utilities so the customer has nothing to do but move in.

If people realized how much they were being charged for these services, they'd never pay them, but we've been trained by the automobile industry to focus on how much it costs per *month*, rather than how much things actually cost. As long as you keep the monthly payments affordable, people don't seem to care how long they'll have to pay a monthly bill.

Homes sold this way seem cheap at the time of purchase, but the difference between manufactured homes and site-built buildings is that manufactured homes are guaranteed to *depreciate* rather than appreciate! To avoid the expensive repairs and the depreciation, you'll want to sell the homes to the tenants before they move in.

With newer and nicer units, you'll be able to charge more per month and attract people with good jobs and few problems. These people are in it for the long term. They see the opportunity to buy the manufactured home as the first step of a three-step plan toward home ownership.

First, they pay for seven or eight years on the newer home. The home will still be in fairly good condition at the end of the payoff because they'll take care of it when it's theirs.

When they have the manufactured home paid off, they can afford to purchase a parcel of land to move the home onto because the money that was being paid to you for the manufactured home can now go toward a land payment with a ten-year or fifteen-year term.

When the land is paid off, the equity in the land should be enough to obtain a construction loan to build a new site built home. By that time, the manufactured home will be about thirty years old, but will still be of value to someone else who is just starting out.

After seven years, your tenants will leave your property to purchase their own land. When this happens, you purchase another manufactured home and start the process all over again!

These units are easy to find and replace compared to other types of real estate. If you buy newer replacement units each time, your property continually looks better and is more valuable.

You'll be earning good money by helping people who want to advance on the economic ladder. Because you're not responsible for any of the maintenance, the checks each month are referred to by the investors who own these properties as "mailbox money"!

The acid test you should apply before purchasing *any* property is this: *would I send my wife or daughter to collect the rent after dark?* (This of course assumes that you *love* your wife or daughter and care about their welfare.) If the answer is "yes," then buy the property. If the answer is "no," look for another property to purchase.

If you feel that an area isn't safe enough for your loved ones to *visit*, who would think that it's safe enough for their loved ones to *live*?

Many times the people who rent in a neighborhood with a lot of drug activity turn out to be participants in the activity who want to be closer to their source of drugs. These types of properties appreciate slower (if at all) and have very high turnover rates.

One of the reasons I recommend that you buy newer units is the mindset of those who choose to live in these older run-down trailers. These people are stuck at the lowest level of our society and they don't like being there.

Most of these people don't know how to get out of the rut they're in and they have virtually no pride of ownership. Their frustrations cause them to blame their circumstances on others. Who is better to blame than "the man" they must pay their rent to every month?

Because this group rarely has much available to put down as a security deposit, they have nothing to lose for leaving your property totally trashed at the end of their stay. A low security deposit yields low accountability. This can cost thousands of dollars if you let it happen, which is why I recommend the purchase of units less than 10 years old. You can charge more in rent, collect a larger security deposit, and attract better tenants.

Condos & Townhomes

Condominiums and townhomes are the first step into home ownership for many people. A condo is typically very similar to an apartment building except that each unit is individually owned. Because the units are in the same building, condos typically have an association that manages the property and pays the water and hazard insurance bills that would be difficult to separate.

During the condo conversion craze from 2004 - 2006, many apartment buildings were converted to condominiums.

These units are nothing more than owner-occupied apartments. Multi-story condominium or apartment complexes are not ideal places to live because you have people walking on your ceiling and their music resonates in your walls.

Conversely, townhomes are often free-standing or built in an arrangement with shared walls but each unit typically owns to the sky, so there are not people living above you.

Many townhomes and condos offer amenities, such as swimming pools, saunas, hot tubs, and tennis courts that people could not afford alone. The price of these types of homes often appeals to young singles and newlyweds who are just starting out on their own.

This is not the most financially stable age group of our society. Many first-time owners quickly outgrow their unit when they have children or get married. The average American lives in a house six or seven years before moving elsewhere. In my experience, young condo owners stay only about a *year and a half* before moving, but condos catering to retirees or professionals often have a much longer term of ownership.

Because of the constant turnover from young condo owners, there are always units identical to yours for sale. When the supply is greater than the demand, properties don't sell quickly, and young people don't generally have the financial ability to wait on the right market that would yield them a higher selling price.

At this stage in their life, they can't afford two mortgage payments for very long, so these sellers tend to quickly reduce their asking price just to get out from under the mortgage. After the sale is recorded, it becomes a comparable sale that will affect the future selling price of other units in the complex. Thus, if you owned a similar unit and needed to sell it quickly, you would need to set your asking price at a level to match those of the previous sales. As a result, it's not uncommon to see condominium units sell for the same price year after year with little or no appreciation.

In addition, as a condo owner, you have no control over the homeowners' association (HOA) dues. It's not uncommon for dues to be over 20% of the monthly mortgage payment (the dues usually include water, property insurance (on the structure), roof repairs, landscaping, and painting of exterior and common hallways). If you didn't have to pay HOA dues each month, you could probably afford to spend $15,000 to $20,000 more on a home mortgage.

Another factor to consider with condo ownership is that utilities are fairly inexpensive since there is often only one wall exposed to the outside elements (the other walls being internal or shared with adjacent condos). Property taxes on condos are usually less expensive than taxes on a single-family home.

Condos generally don't make good rental properties for families. Because most condos don't have private yards, and with many strangers coming and going constantly, families frequently overlook this rental option.

Another factor to consider when evaluating a condo as a potential rental property is whether or not the property offers garages or carports for residents. If someone is a renter, chances are good that their car is the most expensive asset they own. Young professionals who own expensive cars are usually willing to pay higher rents for properties offering garages or carports to protect their car from harsh environmental elements, theft, and vandalism.

Apartment Complexes

Apartment complexes usually have vacancy rates much higher than other residential rental units. But, due to economies of scale, they're relatively inexpensive to build and, therefore, offer a relatively low cost per unit. It's advisable to hire a property manager to manage an apartment complex because the constant turnover, vacancies, and repairs can easily become a full-time job.

Most small investors can't afford large apartment complexes. Fewer buyers for such properties mean a lower demand, which in turn leads to lower sales prices. The return on investment of apartment complexes can be quite high for this reason.

Another factor to consider, as discussed earlier, is that the cost to service the loan debt might be higher for apartment complexes than for other types of properties (lenders tend to charge higher interest rates on loans for properties with more than four units).

If you're contemplating the purchase of an older complex, you'll want to factor in the likely need to hire a maintenance staff. It's become increasingly common to hire a retired couple for this task. This can be an ideal fit for both parties because one spouse typically cleans the pool, maintains the grounds, and makes repairs, while the other maintains the office, pays the bills, and shows vacant apartments.

If you were considering this, you'd want to look for friendly, outgoing people with a strong work ethic and a sense of pride in doing a good job. For their efforts, the couple receives a free place to live and a small salary to enhance their Social Security check.

CHAPTER 7 - PROPERTIES TO CONSIDER

Land

Many old-timers will tell you that land is a good investment because "they're not making any more of it." I agree that land can offer a good, long-term return but there is little opportunity for income (in some cases you may be able to rent the land for agricultural use or as a temporary parking lot). As a result, monthly payments and taxes must be paid out of pocket each year until you sell or refinance the property.

Upside Up™ in Real Life

Subdividing Acreage

In 2005, an eighty-acre parcel of agricultural land in Tucson, AZ was purchased, surveyed, split into five parcels, and sold *four months later* to five unrelated parties for a profit of more than one-million dollars.

Two of my clients purchased one of these parcels, measuring fourteen acres, for $430,000. After subdividing the land into four parcels, they installed a road and a shared well. In less than a year, they'd sold two of the parcels for enough to repay all that they had spent on the project. They decided to keep the other two lots for themselves rather than realize the *half million dollar profit* they'd created.

Increases in land prices are typically caused by external forces that you can't control, so, there is no guarantee that an event that will drive your property value higher will happen soon or happen at all. There may also be events that cause property values to go down.

You may be able to change the intended use of the land, but that usually means changing the zoning, which can be tricky if not impossible. The help of an experienced appraiser can prove invaluable for this process. The only sure-fire way to make money on land is to *develop* it.

Upside Up™ in Real Life

<u>Adjacent Property</u>

In 2004, I was at a friend's home for a party and noticed a vacant lot across the street. I asked who owned it and was informed that the property belonged to a church. Upon checking, I found that the property had commercial zoning and had recently been purchased by a commercial developer.

I told my friends about a subdivision in northwest Tucson that had been built next to a commercial property that for years had been used to store a landscaper's trees and other vegetation. One day, to everyone's surprise, a vehicle-storage facility began operation on the property. It seems that the landscaper had retired and sold the property. The once "natural" view of desert vegetation is now a sea of travel trailers, boats, and horse trailers.

My friends could face a worse situation because the land across from them was zoned to allow a gas station. The high, bright lights and all-night service would be very disruptive to their sleep, especially if the customers filling their car with gas have the volume cranked up on their car stereo to hear their favorite song. My friends decided to sell, rather than worry about what *might* happen on the lot next door.

The value of a residential lot is found by finding the value of surrounding homes and then subtracting the cost to build the homes. If the lot was rezoned and you could build a gas station, the value would be exponentially higher because the value would be determined by the cash flow you could produce on the property.

In many areas, you can build residential buildings on commercial land, but you can't build commercial buildings on residential land. Since commercial property can be adjacent to residential property, you should always check the zoning of vacant land surrounding any residential properties you might consider purchasing. If you're adjacent to a commercial property, it could be developed with an undesirable business and cause your property value to decline substantially.

8

Setting Your Parameters

"Destiny is no matter of chance. It is a matter of choice: It is not a thing to be waited for, it is a thing to be achieved."
– William Jennings Bryan

Return on Investment (ROI)

The return on an investment indicates how well the investment is performing. Before investing, you need to know the amount the investment will earn each year so you can determine whether the benefit is worth the risk.

Calculating the *rate* of return allows you to compare different investment opportunities to one another so you can choose the investment that produces the best return with the least amount of risk.

Risk and reward go hand in hand; you usually don't get one without the other. Before beginning to crunch numbers to calculate how much each investment will earn, you should have *written into your business plan* the minimum return that you're willing to accept. I can't emphasize this enough!

You need to carefully consider the consequences involved with investing. If you take on too much risk, you could lose everything, and if you don't take on enough risk, you won't reach the financial goals you desire.

When you decide on an acceptable level of risk, you should include it in your business plan. It's also a good idea to keep this plan with you when you're looking at property so you won't make decisions based on emotion that don't match your written financial goals.

Your earnings goal should match your personality type; if you're naturally cautious and worry a lot, you'll want safer investments—but this approach typically means lower returns.

If you're aggressive and throw caution to the wind, you'll want to set your earning goal higher, but not so high that you'll never find a property to buy. Remember, you won't earn any money if you don't find a deal! Your investment goal should be achievable and repeatable.

94

CHAPTER 8 - SETTING YOUR PARAMETERS

Your *return on investment* (ROI) can be calculated by dividing the total amount returned to you each year by the total amount you invested.

$$\frac{\text{TOTAL RETURN}}{\text{TOTAL INVESTMENT}} = \text{RETURN ON INVESTMENT (ROI)}$$

Before doing anything else, you'll want to calculate the *total investment* needed to determine whether or not you have enough money to purchase the property you're considering. Total investment can be determined using the following formula:

Down Payment
+ Closing Costs
+ Initial Repairs
_____

TOTAL INVESTMENT

A detailed description of each component in this formula follows.

Down Payment
When purchasing an investment property, most lenders require a borrower to use their own money for at least 10% of the total purchase price. This investment from the borrower is called the *down payment*. This is typically the largest portion of your total investment.

The larger the down payment, the less risk the bank has of losing their money. When a bank experiences less risk, it usually charges a lower interest rate.

For example, let's assume that the purchase price of a property is $200,000. The buyer invests 10% of the purchase price ($20,000) as a down payment, and the bank provides the other 90% ($180,000). If the buyer doesn't make the payments as agreed, the bank will foreclose on the property (take over ownership).

For the bank to lose money, the value of the property must fall below $180,000. Accrued interest, legal fees, and the court costs a that lender must pay to foreclose on a property could easily consume the 10% down payment during the foreclosure process. If the market turns downward (meaning the bank might not be able to sell the property for at least $180,000), the chances of the bank losing money are increased even further.

If instead of a 10% down payment ($20,000), the buyer makes a down payment of 20% ($40,000), then the bank would not experience a loss on the loan unless their foreclosure fees, combined with a loss in property value, were more than $40,000.

Thus, there is usually little risk to the bank with a 20% down payment. The market would have to experience a huge price adjustment for the property value to fall below a sufficient sales price to allow the bank to recover the amount of the loan. Because the chance of this happening is not very likely, the interest rate the bank charges the buyer for the use of their money will be lower in this scenario because the risk to the lender is much lower.

If the borrower obtained a loan for 100% of the property value, the lender would be at risk immediately if the buyer didn't make a payment or the property value declined.

Upside Up™ in Real Life

<u>100-percent Financing</u>

In 2005, loan programs became available that provided 100% financing on investment properties. I'm usually willing to try new investment ideas that *seem* logical, so my wife and I refinanced the garage-conversion property I described earlier in Chapter 2.

The appraised value of this property in 2001 had been $189,000, but four years later it was appraised for $302,000! We obtained 100% financing with a first mortgage for 80% of the property's value and a second mortgage for 20%. After paying for closing costs, we received a check for nearly $153,000.

When we had refinanced in 2001, we received $17,000 more than we'd invested. After refinancing again in 2005, our total cash-out profit to date was almost $170,000!!! But there was a downside.

While the interest rate on the first mortgage was only 7.125%, the 11.875% rate on the second was *painful*! Our substantially higher loan payment turned what had been a *positive* monthly cash flow of $600 into a *negative* cash flow of $650 – a difference of $1,250 per month.

Although the money received from this property has been re-invested into other income-producing opportunities, I wouldn't do this again. In the event we needed to sell in the near future, we'd have to pay the commissions and closing costs out of pocket. I don't advise holding properties with a negative cash flow for a long period of time.

If you're able to obtain 100% financing, you'll pay a much higher interest rate because the lender's risk will have been substantially increased — and lenders hate risk! The higher the risk, the more you pay. When the risk becomes higher than a lender is willing to accept, they simply deny the loan.

With each monthly payment you make, the lender's risk is reduced slightly because the amount of the loan decreases as the borrower makes payments against the principal.

In an appreciating real estate market, the lender's risk is reduced even further because property values are increasing and the loan amount is decreasing relative to the value of the property. In depreciating markets, the lender may require a larger down payment to compensate for decreasing property values.

Closing Costs

Closing costs are the fees the lender requires you to pay before it will issue a loan on the property. Fees paid to the lender and the title company in connection with the loan can cost thousands of dollars. Many of these fees are variable and are determined by the amount of the loan. A summary of the fees you can expect to pay follows:

Lender fees - These costs might include a loan origination fee, loan discount fee (points), appraisal fee, credit report fee, inspection fee, administrative fee, tax service fee, underwriting fee, processing fee, recording fee, escrow fee, wire fees, express mail fees, and mortgage broker fees.

Lender pre-paid items - The lender requires that some items be paid in advance. These include the current month's prorated interest, hazard insurance for one year, taxes, and mortgage insurance (if the down payment is less than 20%).

Lender reserves - The lender also requires reserves to be deposited into an escrow account to pay bills associated with the property. These reserves typically include a few additional months of hazard insurance, mortgage insurance, city and county property taxes, and annual assessments (if there are any).

The lender would assume more risk if these items were unpaid, so they hold your money and pay the fees themselves to be assured that their risk is minimized.

Title and escrow charges - An escrow officer acts as a neutral party in the transaction to ensure that both parties perform the obligations required of them by the contract. The title company conducts a title search and provides insurance to defend the title against future claims or liens.

Title companies earn money for their services with closing fees, title search fees, title examination fees, title insurance fees (for both the lender's and owner's policies), document preparation fees, notary fees, endorsement fees, courier fees, and recording service fees.

Government charges - Any time money is being spent, we can count on state and local governments to get in on the action. Some local municipalities charge transfer fees, recording fees, and tax stamps on each real estate sale. An affidavit of value is signed by both the buyer and seller at closing. This document provides the county tax assessor with the details of every real estate transaction so they can track property values and adjust property taxes (usually upward) for the next tax year.

Additional settlement fees - Other fees related to the purchase are settled at closing. These might include a survey, pest inspection and treatment, homeowners' association transfer fees, bills from contractors for unpaid repairs, and unpaid property taxes.

Initial Repairs

Initial repairs are the property improvements that must be completed before a property can be rented. These repairs include those that would be difficult to complete after a tenant has moved in, or those that are required immediately, such as a leaky roof.

Because these repairs occur *before* any income has been earned, the repair costs need to be added to the down payment and closing costs in order to determine the total cash that will be required to purchase and repair the property.

Your accountant will deduct the cost of these repairs on your income tax return, which will reimburse some of your investment capital. But the initial payment for these repairs must come from your cash reserves before any rent is collected. Ongoing repairs for the property are covered by a *per unit* fee we set aside each month for such purposes.

Total Investment

After determining the amount of down payment, closing costs, and initial repairs you'll need pay, you can quickly calculate whether or not you can afford to purchase a property. It's a good idea to determine this in the beginning, before you spend a lot of time and effort calculating the rents and expenses.

If the amount of cash required for the purchase is more than you have available, you may decide to wait for a project that doesn't require as much money or until you have more saved up. If the project is just too good to pass up, you have several options:

- find an investment partner to share the project

- find a private lender to fund the amount you're short

- find a loan program with a lower down payment

- ask the seller to pay the closing costs and repairs

- find another investor to buy the property (this is referred to as *wholesaling* - you receive a finder's fee for putting the deal together) Check with your attorney to see if this is legal. Finder's fees are *illegal* in Arizona!

Investment Return

After you've established how much money you'll need to invest in the property, you'll want to know how much income your investment will produce (income in this instance refers to the total benefit realized from owning the property).

The income you earn on an investment is also known as the *return*. This is the money that your investment "returns" to you each year in one form or another.

The total return from a property can be calculated by adding the cash flow, principal of the loan(s), and income tax credit or refund that resulted from owning property.

Cash Flow
+ Principal
+ Income Tax Credit/Refund
_____

Total Return

Because rate of return and interest rate are commonly expressed as annual amounts, you also need to express cash flow, principal, and your income tax refund in annual amounts rather than monthly amounts. Each of these items is explained in more detail below:

Cash Flow

Cash flow, for real estate investments, is the amount of income left over after all expenses have been paid. Common expenses for rental properties include mortgage payment(s), property taxes, hazard insurance, and repair costs. I typically include a 5% vacancy reserve as a monthly expense to ensure that the bills can be paid in the event the property is vacant in the future.

If the total expenses are more than the rent collected each month, the property will lose money and you'll need to tap your reserves to pay the bills each month. This is called *negative cash flow*. Taking in more income than is needed to pay the monthly bills is called *positive cash flow*.

Principal

Principal is the amount of the monthly mortgage payment that goes toward paying off the loan. Each month when the mortgage payment is made, a large portion of the payment goes toward interest, the fee we pay to a lender for using their money. The remainder of the payment is applied toward principal, which reduces the amount that you owe on your loan. Principal is usually the only expense on a rental property that is not tax deductible.

Income Tax Credit/Refund

Income tax credit/refund refers to the amount of income tax an investor would not have to pay or would receive as a refund as a result of owning the rental property. Rents collected must be claimed as *income* on an investor's tax return.

All of the expenses associated with the property (except payments toward principal) are subtracted from the total income received, which determines the net rental income. In addition to deductions for expenses, investors are able to deduct an amount for depreciation of the property's improvements.

To maximize your income tax refund you'll need to utilize a knowledgeable accountant. If you prepare your taxes yourself or use a tax accountant who doesn't specialize in investment real estate, you're probably paying too much in taxes.

The expertise of a good accountant can substantially decrease the amount of your income tax obligation. The money saved in income taxes can be substantially higher than the amount you pay to a good accountant for their services.

When you know how much you'll be able to deduct, you can calculate the income tax credit or refund you can expect. In most cases, if you're leveraged properly, your income tax credit/refund will be more than the cash flow of the property.

Property Appreciation

Due to the non-linear nature of appreciation, I never depend on it in my profit expectations for short-term projects unless I'm personally planning to do something to increase the property's value.

When appreciation occurs, I'll gladly accept it. But, it is never *guaranteed* to happen, and in some areas it doesn't. This conservative approach usually causes my investments to perform much better than projected.

I take appreciation into account when it's something that I control, such as adding square footage to a home. If I know the average sale price in a neighborhood is $150 per square foot, and I can build an addition or another house for $100 per square foot, then logically, a $50 per square foot difference is created.

This appreciation isn't produced by external market conditions. The increase in value is *planned for*, not *prayed for*, and happens because of something I do to create value.

Investment Cycle Time

The cycle time of your investment is the time it takes from start to end to complete. At the end of each investment cycle, your initial investment is returned to you, which enables the start of another investment cycle.

The more cycles you can fit into a year, the more profit you'll earn on your investment. A system that can start and end in three months is more desirable than a system that takes a year to complete because it's easier to earn a smaller profit several times than trying to earn a huge profit on one deal.

CHAPTER 8 - SETTING YOUR PARAMETERS

I'd much rather earn $15,000 every three months than $60,000 once per year. Even though it looks like the outcome is the same ($15,000 × 4 cycles = $60,000), it's not.

When your money is returned every few months, you can adjust your investment strategy to account for changes in market conditions before reinvesting. Money invested for a year doesn't offer that opportunity.

The goal of real estate investing is to get your money back as soon as possible so you can invest in something else. The faster you can get your money back, the better the rate of return will be on your investment.

Successful investors find ways to get their money returned without selling the property. If your profit depends on selling the property at a price above what you paid for it, you have a bad plan because market conditions control your outcome. As long as you can find a way to create value that's not dependent on market appreciation, you'll do well.

It's okay to have selling as an *option* in your plan, but the real estate market must be favorable for selling. If your plan *depends* on selling, you'll need to find an alternative during the times that it's not favorable to sell.

Most real estate "investors" aren't investors at all. They're speculators who don't have a plan to create value. Speculators buy properties with the *hope* that they'll increase in value. Investors buy properties because they *plan* to increase the value by changing something.

The speculation strategy sometimes works in a seller's market. But it's a recipe for disaster in a buyer's market when demand changes and properties begin to *depreciate* rather than *appreciate*. This buy-and-pray approach to investing is neither

105

predictable nor repeatable because it depends on external market forces that can't be controlled.

In a free-market economy, supply and demand determine value. Successful investors find a property that is in low demand and quickly transform it into a property that is in high demand by using a repeatable system.

The market is constantly changing. If your system is repeatable but not fast, the market could change drastically between the time you start and end your investment process. The faster you complete your investment, the less chance there is for the market to change and negate all of the assumptions that were made under different market conditions.

9

Projecting
Your Profit

"No man acquires property without acquiring with it a little arithmetic also."– Ralph Waldo Emerson

Property Analysis

To calculate how well (or badly) an investment is going to perform, I developed the *Rental Property Analysis Worksheet* in Table 9-1. This worksheet can help you calculate the income, expenses, depreciation, and rate of return on properties you're considering for purchase.

You'll need to make some initial assumptions in order to complete the worksheet. As you make each assumption, be sure to write it down on a separate sheet of paper. If your offer is accepted, you'll need to verify all of the assumptions on this *Assumption Sheet* while performing your due diligence during the inspection period.

Purchase Information

The first section at the top of the worksheet is titled *Purchase Information.* This section includes general information about the property, assumptions about your income tax rates, and information about your loan.

Property Address - It's very easy to mix these sheets up after you've run several of them, so always start by entering the property address.

Purchase Price - Enter the amount of the purchase price. I always enter the asking price, because it's usually a safe assumption that the seller would accept a full price offer. If the numbers don't work at the asking price, you can enter a lower purchase price later and rerun the numbers.

Table 9-1 Rental Property Analysis Worksheet

PURCHASE INFORMATION	PROPERTY ADDRESS:			
	Amount	% of Sales Price	Federal INCOME TAX % State	
Purchase Price		100%		
Down Payment			Interest Rate	Term (years)
1st Mortgage				
2nd Mortgage (or seller carry back)				
CASH REQUIRED	Amount	PROPERTY VALUATION		VACANCY RATE
Down Payment		Land (usually 20%)		
Closing Costs (about 3% of 1st mortgage amount)		Improvements		
Amount of Initial Fix-up Required		DEPRECIATION	Residential (yrs)	Commercial (yrs)
Total Investment			27.5	39

INCOME	CURRENT		PROJECTED	
	Annual	Monthly	Annual	Monthly
Gross Rents				
Other Income (laundry, billboard, etc.)				
less vacancy rate (typically 5%)				
Adjusted Gross Rent (AGR)				

EXPENSES	CURRENT		PROJECTED	
	Annual	Monthly	Annual	Monthly
Principal (1st Mortgage)				
Interest (1st Mortgage)				
Principal (2nd Mortgage)				
Interest (2nd Mortgage)				
Total Debt Service (should be 50% of AGR or less)				
Property Taxes				
Insurance				
Water & Sewer				
Gas & Electric				
Repairs				
Misc. Expenses (ads, phone, mileage, etc.)				
Total Non-Debt Expenses (30%-40% of AGR)				
TOTAL EXPENSES (Debt Service + Other Exp.)				
NET RENT (CASH FLOW) (Adjusted Gross Rent - Total Expenses)				

INCOME TAX CONSEQUENCES	CURRENT		PROJECTED	
	Annual	Monthly	Annual	Monthly
Income (Adjusted Gross Rent)				
less Expenses (Total Expenses - Principal)				
less Depreciation (Improvements ÷ 27.5 years)				
less Uncaptured Expenses (closing costs, capital equip. etc.)				
Total Tax Deduction				
TAX REFUND (Tax Deduction × Income Tax %)				

RETURN ON INVESTMENT (ROI) (Net Rent+Principal+Tax Refund) ÷ Total Invested		

Income Tax Rate - Enter your federal and state income tax percentages. Use the highest tax rate that you pay, because your tax refund will be calculated at the highest rate you pay until you reach an income level that puts you in the next lowest tax bracket. Income tax rates for the United States can be found at *www.irs.gov*.

Let's assume that your highest tax rate is 25% and your state income tax is calculated at 14% of the tax rate you pay in federal income tax. Enter 25% in the left-hand tax column, and 3.5% in the right-hand tax column (.14 × .25 = .035 or 3.5%).

Down Payment - By now you should have been pre-qualified for a loan by a mortgage lender. The lender should have informed you of the various loan programs it offers and the amount of down payment that is required by each.

Enter the amount of down payment you plan to pay on your purchase and the percentage the down payment is of the total. For example, if the asking price of the property is $200,000, and you plan to invest $20,000 as a down payment, enter $20,000 in the *Amount* column, and 10% in the *% of Sales Price* column.

First Mortgage – Enter the amount that you plan to borrow from your mortgage lender on the property. For example, if the asking price of the property is $200,000, and you plan to borrow 80%, then enter $160,000 in the *Amount* column, and 80% in the *% of Sales Price* column.

Second Mortgage - If you plan to obtain a second mortgage, or a loan from the seller, known as a *seller carry-back*, enter the amount you intend to borrow in a second-position loan. For example, if the asking price of the property is $200,000, and you plan to obtain a second mortgage of 10% of the purchase price, then enter $20,000 in the *Amount* column, and 10% in the *% of Sales Price* column.

Interest Rate and Term (of Loan) - To the right of the columns for the first and second mortgage, you'll find a section to enter your financing assumptions for this property. If you've already been pre-qualified by a lender, you should have a pretty good idea of the loan program that best fits your needs.

You'll need to know the rate of interest being charged and the number of years it will take to repay the loan. If you plan to obtain two loans, enter the rate and term for each loan in the appropriate spaces.

The rate and term for the first mortgage is entered in the first row of this section and the second mortgage (if there is one) would be entered in the row directly beneath the first mortgage.

Cash Required

The second section of the Rental Property Analysis Worksheet will help you to add up all of the money you'll need to pay before the property begins to produce income.

Down Payment - The down payment for this section should be the same as the down payment assumed in the first section. You're entering it again to put all of the up-front expenses together so you won't forget to include any of them.

Closing Costs - When you purchase a property in the United States, lenders require that you provide a title policy from the American Land Title Association (ALTA). This policy, often called an *ALTA policy*, protects your lender's interest in the property and provides more coverage than a typical owner's title policy. The expanded coverage for the lender includes liens that may not be found in the public record.

Other expenses may include loan origination fees, processing fees, administrative fees, recording fees, courier fees, and overnight delivery fees. The amount you spend in fees varies by lender and loan program. Look for a lender who has competitive rates, can close the loan on time, and offers low fees.

Once paid, loan fees are gone forever, so shop around to find a good lender. These fees typically don't exceed 3% of the loan amount, so use 3% as a safe estimate for closing costs.

Initial Fix-up Required - This entry is intended to capture the cost of the repairs that are necessary before a property can be rented. If you have plans to improve the property between the time you purchase it and the time your tenant moves in, then estimate the total cost of the improvements and enter it in this row of the *Amount* column.

Total Investment - The total of your down payment, closing costs, and initial fix-up costs is the amount of cash you'll need to have available before your first rent check comes in. If you believe it will take a while to find a tenant, you'll also need to add the recurring expenses for the mortgage and utilities to your calculations.

Property Valuation - Your accountant can help you determine the percentage of the purchase price that should be allocated as land value.

This information will be needed later when you calculate depreciation for your income tax return (you can't depreciate land). I typically assume 20% is land and 80% is improvements, but your market area may be different, so check with your accountant.

Vacancy Rate - On the far right-hand side of this section, you'll find a *Vacancy Rate* column. No matter how good of a landlord you are, sooner or later, you'll have a vacancy. Because vacancy is inevitable, you need to plan for it in your numbers. I typically assume 5% vacancy, which means that each of my units will be empty about 18 days each year (365 days/year × 5% = 18.25 days/year).

Depreciation Rate - The last entry in this section is for the depreciation rate allowed by the government. In the United States, a residential property is depreciated over a 27.5 year period and a commercial property is depreciated over a 39 year period. Enter the appropriate rate that applies for the property you intend to purchase.

Income

From this point forward, the worksheet is split into two major headings for income: Current and Projected.

The *Current* column is for all of the current income, expense, and income tax information. Prior to purchasing any property, you should have a written plan of how you'll increase the property's value. This can usually be done by adding square footage, changing the use, or adding amenities.

The *Projected* column is provided to calculate the anticipated results of your changes. The *Current* and *Projected* columns are broken down further into *Annual* and *Monthly* columns. You'll need to use both annual and monthly entries because some items are commonly expressed in months and others are expressed in years.

For example, rents and utility bills are usually paid each month, but expenses, such as hazard insurance and property taxes, are paid annually.

When running mathematical calculations, variables must be converted to the same increments before adding or subtracting can be completed. You'll need to view the income and expenses in *months* to ensure that you'll be able to pay the bills as they come in. But, you'll also need to calculate income and expenses in *years* in order to file your income taxes and calculate your profit.

Gross Rents - The total rent you receive before deducting expenses is your gross rent. If you advertised your property for rent at $18,000 per year, your phone probably wouldn't ring very much. Rent of $1,500 per month works out to the same annual total, but sounds a lot more affordable than $18,000. Enter both the monthly and annual amounts for each income and expense item on your worksheet; you'll need them later.

Don't forget also to add the monthly rent to your assumption list. If your offer is accepted, you'll have time during your due diligence period to verify that you'll be able to obtain the assumed monthly rent.

CHAPTER 9 - PROJECTING YOUR PROFIT

One of the best ways to find out how much other properties with similar amenities are renting for is to call on ads and drive around to see what else is available. You must know what other landlords are charging to ensure that your rents will be competitive and your property won't remain vacant for long periods of time.

Other Income - This space is for non-rent income produced by the property you're considering. The most common examples include coin-operated laundry facilities, arcade games, or vending machines. Less common examples include properties along major highways that receive billboard income for having large signs on their land, and revenue from cellular telephone companies for providing a place for their antennas.

If a property has non-rent income, enter both the annual and monthly amount in the space for *Other Income* on the worksheet.

Adjusted Gross Rents - The Adjusted Gross Rent (AGR) is the amount of rent that's left after deducting for vacancy. To find the AGR, add the rental income to the non-rental income and subtract the amount you allocated for vacancy. The remaining income after vacancy is needed to calculate cash flow after all expenses have been accounted for.

Expenses

The expenses you likely will incur include those related to the repayment of the mortgage (principal, interest, taxes, and insurance), as well as for utilities, repairs, and other miscellaneous expenses.

Principal and Interest - The largest expense for most landlords is the mortgage payment they make to the bank each month. In the early stages of a long-term mortgage, the interest portion of the payment is much higher than the amount you pay toward the principal. As each monthly payment is made, the principal portion becomes a bit higher and the interest portion a bit lower.

Most monthly payments to banks include principal, interest, taxes, and insurance (or, *PITI*). Even though you probably write one check to the bank for all of these things, you must isolate each item in order to calculate your income taxes.

Enter the principal and interest for each loan in the space provided. Use a financial calculator with an amortization function to compute the interest and principal for each loan in both months and years. The total of all interest and principal payments made on your loan(s) is called your *debt service*.

To ensure that your property will produce an adequate profit, the debt service should be 50% or less of the Adjusted Gross Rent (AGR) previously calculated.

Don't forget that you'll also need to pay taxes, hazard insurance, repairs, maintenance, and HOA fees. You'll need to ensure that after paying all of these expenses, there is money left over for a profit.

If the debt service is more than the AGR, this would be a good place to stop running numbers and *run away* from the property. You might as well stand on a street corner handing out one hundred dollar bills to strangers. The end result will be the same, and you'll spend much less time getting rid of the money!

CHAPTER 9 - PROJECTING YOUR PROFIT

Property Taxes - Property taxes have always been a matter of public record. In the past, tax information was rather cumbersome to obtain, but many municipalities have computerized their tax rolls and provide 24-hour access to the information on their Internet website. To determine the annual taxes, contact your local tax assessor to get either the website address or the tax data. Calculate the taxes in both months and years and enter the amounts in the appropriate line on the worksheet.

Hazard Insurance - The current owner of the property you're considering for purchase probably has hazard insurance coverage, but you'll need to check with your own insurance agent to find how much *your* premium will be. Be sure to also check whether the property requires flood insurance.

If flood insurance is required, add the premium to that of the hazard insurance before entering the monthly and annual amount in the worksheet. Sometimes new buildings or additions are not allowed on properties in a floodplain, so be sure to check with the engineering department at your local public works building.

To protect against insurance fraud, the insurance industry has created a national database called the Comprehensive Loss Underwriting Exchange (CLUE). This database contains the complete history of insurance claims made in recent years. The insurance companies can search this database by property or by person to avoid issuing insurance on properties or to people with several claims. During your due diligence, it's advisable to obtain a CLUE report on the property you're considering or at a minimum, a claims history from the current owner.

117

Upside Up™ in Real Life

Water Claims

One of my clients was dropped by their insurance company a few weeks after closing on their home. It seems their insurance carrier found that two water-damage claims had been made against the property by the previous owners.

As it turns out, one of the claims was due to a double patio door blowing open during a rainstorm and the other, due to an evaporative cooler leak that introduced water into the ductwork. Neither claim was due to flooding or roof issues, but it took a lot of explaining to get the insurance reinstated.

Public Utilities - Many public utility companies will provide annual billing information for natural gas, electricity, water, and sewer over the telephone. If they will not provide the information, request copies of the bills for the past 12 months from the current owner.

Even if the tenants pay their own utilities, you'll want to obtain this information because tenants don't like high utility bills any more than you do. You'll have frequent turnover if the utility bills are too high. Excessive water or gas bills may indicate a leak that has gone undetected or is being hidden by the current owner. When all of the utility billing information has been gathered, enter the monthly and annual amount of each in your worksheet and look for abnormally high or low entries.

Repairs - I've met investors who use a percentage of the sales price to calculate their repairs. But, I've found that calculating repairs by the number of units is more reliable than by the price you pay for the property. Each unit has a stove, dishwasher, air conditioner, and furnace that will need to be replaced over time.

For my calculations, I plan to spend $50 per unit per month for repairs unless the building is brand new. It's been my experience that this method works well on all property types, except mobile homes, which would need a larger allotment set aside.

The money for your repair budget should be subtracted from the rent each month and placed in a separate bank account. Your vacancy allotment should also go into this separate account each month. Failure to do this will create havoc when several units are vacant and you have to replace an air conditioner or two in the same month. You won't want to take out an equity loan on your home to cover these expenses, so *plan* for them by pretending that they happen each month!

Miscellaneous Expenses - The last expense category is for all expenses that haven't been captured elsewhere. For example, because you plan to have vacancy of 5% or more, you'll probably need to spend money to advertise and show your property. Estimate how many miles you'll need to drive, how many calls on your cellular phone you'll need to take, and how much you'll need to spend to re-rent the property.

Non-debt Expenses - The total of all expenses other than principal and interest is called *non-debt expenses*. These expenses typically consume between 30% and 40% of the AGR. Add the non-debt expenses to the total debt service to find the total expenses you can expect to pay monthly and yearly for the property.

Net Rent (Cash Flow) - Once you've calculated the total rent after vacancy and the total expenses, you can determine whether the property will produce an income or a loss each month.

You should start investing in properties that produce a *positive* cash flow, unless you're going into business to become a charity. After you own several income-producing properties, you can consider the purchase of a property that loses money because of possible longer-term advantages of doing so.

Many times, properties in high-demand areas can't generate enough rental income to pay their expenses. This is usually due to the high cost of purchasing the property. Because of the high demand for these properties, they usually appreciate at a faster rate than properties in other areas.

These properties can be good long-term investments, as long as you have other properties to pay for the deficit each month. Appreciation happens over long periods of time, so you must be prepared to wait for years until the time is right to sell. I wouldn't purchase properties like this unless I could do something to them to create value.

Income Tax Consequences

The amount of your income tax refund (or a reduction in the amount you owe) depends on your income, your tax rate, the number of the deductions you're able to claim, and whether the properties you own produce positive or negative cash flow. Mortgage interest is usually the largest expense on leveraged properties (i.e., for those purchased with a loan).

Because such a significant portion of the rent is going to pay interest, it's not unusual for your income tax refund to be higher than the cash flow produced by these properties.

AGR and Total Expenses - Income tax is computed annually, so you need to use the annual numbers from your previous calculations. Start by entering the *Adjusted Gross Rent* in the appropriate column of the worksheet. Next, enter the *Total Expenses* less the amount that was paid against principal on the first and second mortgages (remember, principal is not deductible).

Depreciation - Depreciation can be calculated by multiplying the purchase price by the percentage of the property that was deemed to be *improvements* (not land) and then dividing by the number of years in the depreciation schedule. Enter the amount of depreciation in the appropriate column.

For example, a $200,000 purchase price × 80% (value of property improvements) ÷ 27.5 years would produce an annual depreciation expense of $5,818.18.

After calculating the annual depreciation, enter it in the worksheet in the appropriate space.

Uncaptured Expenses – Expenses that are deducted over the life of your loan—rather than being deducted in the year the expenditure took place—are called *uncaptured expenses*. Under current U.S. tax laws, some closing costs cannot be deducted the year you pay them; rather, they must be equally spread over the life of the loan.

121

For example, if the closing costs are $4,800 on a 30 year loan, the costs would be allocated evenly over a thirty year period. In this case, the closing costs would be divided by 30 years to find the total deduction for each year ($4,800 ÷ 30 years = $160 per year).

Total Tax Deduction - To calculate your income tax deduction, subtract the total expenses, depreciation, and uncaptured expenses from the adjusted gross rent, then add the principal from your loan(s) (AGR – Total Expenses – Depreciation – Uncaptured Expenses + Principal (Loan1) + Principal (Loan2) = Total Tax Deduction. (If you didn't include loan principal as an expense, you don't need to add it into the above equation.)

The bottom line is that even though a property might produce a positive cash flow each year, you can usually show a loss on your income taxes because of being able to claim depreciation!

Note: If you eventually sell the property, you will need to factor in the total amount you deducted for depreciation from your income taxes to be able to calculate your capital gains on the property. To fully understand the implications of the depreciation deduction, you should consult with your tax advisor or accountant.

Tax Refund / Tax Credit - Your income tax refund or income tax credit can be calculated easily by multiplying the *Total Tax Deduction* by the income tax bracket you fall into. If you pay both federal and state income taxes, you'll need to multiply the *Total Tax Deduction* by each tax rate and then add the totals together.

122

For example: ($5,440 Total Tax Deduction × 28% Federal Tax Rate = $1,523.20 refunded) and ($5,440 Total Tax Deduction × 4% State Tax Rate = $217.60 refunded). ($1,523.20 + $217.60 = $1,740.80 Total Refund).

Return on Investment (ROI)

ROI provides us with the annual net profit we earn on our money after taxes. To calculate the *Return on Investment (ROI)*, divide the *Total Return* (Cash Flow + Principal + Income Tax Refund) by the *Total Investment* (Down Payment + Closing Costs + Initial Repairs).

$$\frac{\text{Cash Flow} + \text{Principal} + \text{Income Tax Refund}}{\text{Down Payment} + \text{Closing Costs} + \text{Initial Repairs}} = \text{ROI}$$

Because you have the ability to obtain leveraged ownership by financing, claim a depreciation loss on your income taxes, and receive rental payments each month, it's difficult for other investments to match the rate of return produced by good real estate investments.

10

Learning
About Loans

"Time is like money, the less we have of it to spare the further we make it go."– Josh Billings

Banks earn a good deal of their profit from real estate lending. Besides the interest they earn on the loan, they also profit from fees for originating the loan, preparing the documents, and processing the paperwork. When a bank runs out of money to lend, they sell some of the loans they've made to other banks.

The money received from selling the loans gives the bank more money to lend. Banks want to lend you money; they're in business to provide loans. The more loans they generate, the more profit they earn for their shareholders.

Real estate is considered to be a stable investment that doesn't fluctuate daily like the stock market does. In fact, many banks are willing to lend 90% (sometimes 100%) of a property's value.

Most real estate investors pay 10% or more of the purchase price in cash as their down payment and then borrow the remaining money from a bank. After experiencing huge mortgage losses in 2007, however, many lenders increased their down payment requirement for investors to 20% of the purchase price or more.

From the bank's point of view, a down payment of 20% makes the loan a very safe investment because the property value must fall 20% before the bank begins to lose money. From the investor's point of view this is a good deal too. By investing only a small portion of the property's value, the investor gets to keep 100% of the gain when the property value increases.

Choosing Your Interest Rate

One of the biggest mistakes people make when they purchase rental property is the way they choose their loan program. Most people I know focus on the interest rate rather than the closing costs they must pay to obtain the loan. Due to their fear of what the future may hold, many people choose to lock the interest rate for 30 years so their payments can't change. This security can cost tens of thousands of dollars!

The difference that variations in interest rate and loan length can make on a monthly mortgage payment is illustrated in Table 10-1. The payments shown are for a $1,000 loan amortized over a 15, 20, 25, and 30 year period.

Table 10-1 Monthly Payment for Each $1,000 Borrowed

Interest Rate	15 Years	20 Years	25 Years	30 Years
6.00%	$8.44	$7.16	$6.44	$6.00
6.50%	$8.71	$7.46	$6.75	$6.32
7.00%	$8.99	$7.75	$7.07	$6.65
7.50%	$9.27	$8.06	$7.39	$6.99
8.00%	$9.56	$8.36	$7.72	$7.34
8.50%	$9.85	$8.68	$8.05	$7.69
9.00%	$10.14	$9.00	$8.39	$8.05
9.50%	$10.44	$9.32	$8.74	$8.41
10.00%	$10.75	$9.65	$9.09	$8.78
10.50%	$11.05	$9.98	$9.44	$9.15
11.00%	$11.37	$10.32	$9.80	$9.52
11.50%	$11.68	$10.66	$10.16	$9.90
12.00%	$12.00	$11.01	$10.53	$10.29

Simply multiply the payment that corresponds to your interest rate and loan period times the number of thousands that you owe.

For example: if you owe $246,000, multiply the loan payment by 246 to find your payment.

Upside Up™ in Real Life

<u>Choosing an Interest Rate</u>

When we purchased a new home in 2003, we had the choice between a 4% adjustable rate mortgage (ARM) and a 5½% fixed-rate loan. The monthly payment on the fixed-rate loan was $500 more than the ARM.

The 4% rate was guaranteed to be locked for five years and then would adjust each year to align with the market. The interest rate change was limited to 2% per year, with a maximum increase of 6% over the life of the loan.

Because the rate was locked at 4% for the first five years, we were *guaranteed* to save $500 per month for at least five years. The $30,000 saved in the first five years is enough to cover six *additional* years of increased payments if the rate goes from 4% to 6% after the five-year lock expires.

We didn't need the security of a fixed-rate for *thirty* years because we knew that on average, people move every six or seven years.

In the *Upside Up™ in Real Life* example above, if we deposit the $30,000 saved on our mortgage during the first five years into an investment that earns 10% annually, we'll earn $3,000 per year for the rest of our lives!

On our loan amount of $400,000, an interest rate increase from 4% to 6% would add an additional $8,000 in interest each year. Because the $30,000 that we would save could earn $3,000 per year, the net increase would be only $5,000 ($8,000 - $3,000 = $5,000). If our rate were to stay at 6%, the money saved during the first five years would last an additional six years ($30,000 ÷ $5,000 per year in additional interest = 6 years).

This means that we could live in the property for 11 years before the savings during the first five years are used up. I've never owned a property for more than eight years, so I'm pretty certain that we'll come out ahead on our gamble. If we stay longer, we can refinance our loan if the rate gets too high.

Long-term vs. Short-term Financing

The length of time you plan to hold a property will determine the appropriate amount of your down payment. Mortgage insurance is often required if the down payment is lower than 20% of appraised value. To avoid paying this added expense, many people obtain two loans; a first mortgage for 80% of the value and a second mortgage for 10%, 15%, or 20% of the value.

On a property that you don't intend to own for long, you may decide to put very little down and pay the private mortgage insurance premium rather than obtaining two loans that cost more to originate.

Another alternative on short-term projects is to pay cash. Most people don't have enough money lying around to buy a house, but if you partner with other investors and borrow from your 401(k) accounts, you'd be surprised how much capital you can raise, and how quickly. For a short-term loan, paying cash often makes more sense than obtaining bank financing due to the amount of money you'll save on financing fees.

These fees often work out to two or three percent of the loan amount. When you factor the fees into your interest rate, it would be like adding two or three percentage points to your interest rate during the first year. If you plan to repay the loan in a month, the fees would be substantially higher than the interest you paid because the amount of the fees would stay the same, but the length of time would be reduced to one-twelfth!

For example, on a loan of $100,000, financing fees of 3% would be $3,000 ($100,000 × .03 = $3,000). If the financing fees were spread over one year, it would cost $250 per month to obtain the loan ($3,000 ÷ 12 months = $250 per month).

If you paid the loan off in one month instead of one year, the fees would still be $3,000, but would have cost you $3,000 per month instead of $250 per month. When annualized (converted to years), the closing fees on this one-month loan would equal 36% of the loan amount, and we still haven't calculated the interest!

A loan of $100,000 at 8% simple interest would cost $8,000 per year ($100,000 × .08 = $8,000). When divided by twelve months, the interest payment works out to about $667 per month ($8,000 ÷ 12 months = $666.67 per month). On this short-term loan, the closing costs for one month are almost *five times higher* than the interest! If you add the closing costs and the interest, the combined annual rate on a one month loan is 36.67% (36% + .67% = 36.67%)!

Financing fees are a *fixed* cost. Once paid, the fees are gone forever. The lender won't reimburse them even if you repay the loan the next day. Interest rates are *variable*. The *rate* of interest stays the same whether you pay the loan off in a month or in thirty years, but the *amount* of interest you pay increases every day. Interest accrual directly coincides with how long you use the money.

If you plan to sell a property within a few months of buying it, the interest rate doesn't make much of a difference, but over an extended period of several years, the difference in interest rates will make a huge difference on your outcome!

Upside Up™ in Real Life

Financing With "Hard Money"

In 2007, I bought a home from one of my customers to enable them to purchase a new home. I was able to re-sell the home after owning it for only *twenty-three* days, but the financing turned out to be very costly for the amount of time I used the money.

Because I paid the loan off so fast, the lender earned very little in *interest*, but received more than $4,000 in *fees*. When the cost of the loan is annualized, the fees are equivalent to *twenty percent* of the loan amount (not including interest)!

For a short-term purchase such as this, it would have been much wiser to pay twelve or fifteen percent for a hard money loan from a private investor!

Short-term loan example - On a short-term loan of $100,000, the *difference* between an 8% rate of interest and a 10% rate of interest would be $2,000 for an entire year ($100,000 loan × .02 difference = $2,000). If instead of taking a year to pay off the loan, you paid the loan off in three months (one fourth the time), the difference in interest would only be $500 ($2,000 ÷ 4 = $500). On a short-term loan, I'd much rather pay a higher interest rate than a lot of bank fees, since I'd only be making a few interest payments before paying off the loan.

Long-term loan example - On a long-term loan of $100,000, the difference between an 8% rate of interest and a 10% rate of interest would still be $2,000 per year ($100,000 x.02 difference = $2,000), but if you took *30 years* to pay off the loan, the difference in interest at 10% would be $60,000 *more* than the interest at 8% ($2,000 × 30 = $60,000). On a long-term loan, getting a better interest rate is more important than reducing the lender's fees. Because the bank fees are spread over many years, they have little effect on the rate.

Discount Points

Banks offer the ability to buy down your interest rate with *points*. One point is equal to one percent of your loan amount. For example, on a loan of $100,000, one-percent would be equal to $1,000. To reduce your interest rate by ⅛%, you must pay one percent of the loan amount to the lender.

If you remember nothing else in this entire text, remember this: *points are bad!* Discount points are nothing more than prepaid interest. They are paid up front at the time your loan is issued and it usually takes six or seven years for your savings from the lower monthly payments to reach the amount you paid in advance.

Do you think it's a coincidence that the average person moves every six to seven years? The banks are counting on it! They know that the odds are in their favor that you'll move or refinance before the money they've collected up front is recovered by lower payments.

Who can predict the future seven years from now? Job transfers and family commitments can change in the blink of an eye. If you've paid to buy your rate down and then decide to move six months later, the bank keeps your money and, rather than saving money, you will have spent thousands of dollars needlessly.

You would have to pay the bank $8,000 in advance to lower your interest rate by ½% on a $200,000 loan (one percent of the loan amount for every ⅛% drop in interest rate).

The savings equate to $1,000 per year or about $83 per month ($200,000 × ½% = $1,000 ÷ 12 months = $83.33). If you had to move six months later, none of your $8,000 would be returned to you, which means the cost of saving $83 per month would be $1,333 per month! ($8,000 ÷ 6 months = $1,333.33).

Chances are good that you'll either refinance or move long before you recover the cost of buying down your rate to save interest. Don't forget that mortgage interest is a tax deductible expense, so you'll get a portion of the interest you pay returned in the form of an income tax refund. This is yet another reason not to pay points. *Points are bad!*

Other Lender Fees

In recent years, homeowners have been inundated with unexpected fees at the closing table. Many of these "junk" fees are just ways for lenders to make extra money on each loan. Below are some of the *legitimate* fees a lender might charge.

Document preparation - Someone prepared (typed, copied, collated) the documents for your loan.

Appraisal review - A bank employee reviewed your appraisal report, (which you probably paid for separately) to be sure that your house is worth more than the loan amount and that the neighborhood is not in a state of decline.

Credit report review - A bank employee reviewed your credit report to determine whether or not you're a deadbeat. They also calculated the debt-to-income ratio for all of your recurring loans (how much of your gross income is committed to debt service each month).

Application fee - The amount you pay to apply for a loan. Many borrowers don't follow through with obtaining a loan after taking up several hours of the lender's time. An application fee is charged to compensate for this and the fee paid by the lender to obtain a credit report on the borrower. Some lenders reimburse this fee to the borrowers if they follow through with obtaining a loan.

Processing fee - The fee charged to make copies of the stack of documents you made copies of before you gave them to the bank. A loan package is like a huge jigsaw puzzle that someone must go through to verify your income, assets, and debts. The list of items required by the bank often includes your entire life history—except for baby pictures!

Underwriting fee - The fee for the bank's underwriter to review the reams of documents listed above (pay stubs, bank statements, 401(k) accounts, etc.) and run a software program that tells them whether or not you qualify for the loan.

Overnight mail fee - Some overnight mail fees are legitimate and necessary to get paperwork and funding to or from an out-of-town lender, but watch out! Sometimes the fees are marked up by as much as 300%!

Courier fee - This fee is charged to transport the original signed documents to the County Recorder's office.

Recording fee - This is the fee charged by the County Recorder to scan the documents and catalog them so a future property search will find the liens and sale information related to your transaction.

Understanding Your FICO Score

For years, credit scoring has been a part of the loan underwriting process, but until recently, borrowers weren't allowed to know how their credit scores were computed. By understanding how their score is calculated, buyers can better understand what they can do to improve their credit rating. Though the scoring criteria are generally known, some of the details of this credit scoring system are intentionally vague in order to keep people from exploiting the system.

Background information - Fair Isaac and Co. (FICO) worked with insurance companies to predict the propensity of risk for various activities. The banking industry requested that they also develop a way to score credit that would rate the propensity of loan default by different borrowers.

The *FICO* score computed is a snapshot of a person's credit at the time they're applying for a loan. FICO scores are used by lenders in the United States to make millions of credit decisions each year.

After complaints from both lenders and governmental agencies, FICO released to the public a comprehensive explanation of the factors considered to generate a FICO score and how each element affects the overall credit score.

Higher credit ratings often result in a lower interest rate, which in turn reduces the payment and increases the amount that the homebuyer can qualify to borrow. Derogatory information reflected in your credit report could make the difference of whether or not you're approved to buy a home.

The following factors are evaluated when your credit score is computed: your payment history, the total amount you owe, the length of time your credit history covers, and the number and types of new credit accounts established.

Payment history (35% of score) - how you pay your debts; these factors are considered:

- presence of adverse public records (such as bankruptcy, judgments, lawsuits, liens, or wage attachments), collection items, and/or delinquency items (late)
- amount and severity of delinquency (how late)
- number of past-due items on file
- number of accounts paid as agreed

Amount owed (30% of score) – total outstanding debt; variables considered include:

- amount owed on specific types of accounts
- number of accounts with balances
- proportion of credit lines used, as well as installment loan amounts (including proportion of balances to total credit limits on certain types of revolving accounts and proportion of balance to original loan amount on certain types of installment loans

Length of established credit (15% of score) – how long you've had an established line of credit. NOTE: If parents add their children to an account they've had open for many years, it's possible for the children to have thirty years of credit history when they're only twenty years old!

New credit (10% of score) – includes credit lines that have not been active long enough to establish a credit history:
- number of recently opened accounts, proportion of accounts that are recent, and type of account
- number of recent credit inquiries

Types of credit established (10% of score) – the type of credit you hold, including the number of (presence, prevalence, and recent information on) various types of accounts, such as credit cards, retail accounts, installment loans, mortgages, and consumer finance accounts

For complete information about the credit scoring process, visit the FICO website at *www.fairisaac.com*.

The Five C's of Credit

When determining whether or not to approve your conventional loan, lenders evaluate these five aspects of your credit application: your character and credit history, your capacity to make the payments, your capital assets and collateral, and other conditions or factors.

Character (credit history; minimum FICO score of 620) - Maintaining a good credit history is absolutely crucial. You can finance properties with no money, but you can't finance anything without credit. If you're habitually late, either set your bills up to be paid automatically or pay them a month in advance. One inadvertent late payment to a lender can abruptly end your borrowing ability for six months or more.

Capacity (job stability and income) – Your capacity is your ability to repay the loans you have outstanding. If you're in an unstable job or have more debt than lenders like to see, you may not do well in this category. When people spend money as fast as they earn it or have a sporadic job history, banks won't lend to them until these problems have been corrected.

Capital (assets) – Your net worth is the total of all your assets minus all your liabilities (debts). Banks like to lend to borrowers who have several other assets that could be sold in an emergency in order to make their payments on time. The more net worth you have, the more willing the banks are to lend to you because you've demonstrated the ability to save and that you are financially responsible.

Collateral (value of the property) – The asset that the bank puts a lien on is called the *collateral*. On a mortgage, the collateral is the property, on a vehicle loan, the collateral is the car. Holding collateral gives the lender recourse. In the event the loan is not repaid as promised, the lender can take ownership of the asset that was used to secure the loan.

Conditions (external factors, for example, the economy) – If a major employer is closing down in an area or the housing market is very soft, lenders may tighten their lending standards until they can get a sense of how the local economy will be affected.

Many union employees who are getting close to a strike deadline take out an equity loan on their home before the strike. Lenders will not issue a loan after the strike is called because the borrowers don't have the ability to repay it.

Documentation Required for a Loan

When you apply for a loan, the lender will want to find out everything about you to ensure that you'll be able to repay your loan obligation as agreed.

The following list of documents is typically required at the time your loan application is submitted. Incomplete applications are often set aside until *all* of the information is turned in, so be thorough when gathering the information required by the lender. Use the checklist below to prepare an information package for your lender.

☐ W-2s for the past two (2) years; all borrowers/all jobs

☐ Pay stubs for the most recent month of employment (all borrowers/all jobs, 30 days minimum)

☐ Signed Federal income tax returns (Form 1040), with all schedules, for the past two (2) years. If borrower and/or co-borrower own(s) 25% or more of any business, also provide business tax returns. Self-employed borrowers may be required to supply a year-to-date profit-and-loss statement.

☐ Asset account statements (all pages) for the most recent two (2) months (including checking, savings, and money–market accounts; investment accounts for stocks and bonds;

other asset accounts). Internet printouts are usually acceptable, but borrower name, account number, and financial institution must be shown on all pages. If you're providing account statement printouts from your bank they must be signed and stamped by the teller.

☐ Most recent retirement statement(s) (<u>all</u> pages) for all borrower's 401(k), pensions, and annuities. If the statement is sent monthly, provide most recent two (2) months

☐ Most current mortgage, tax, and insurance statements for <u>all</u> properties owned

☐ If renting, provide current landlord's name, address, and telephone number or 12 consecutive months of cancelled rent checks.

☐ Current and updated lease for all rental properties

☐ Copies of separation or divorce decree, support order, and property settlement agreement, if applicable

☐ If you're using child support or alimony to qualify, you must show a one (1) year history printout from the Domestic Relations Department (or equivalent agency) indicating that you consistently receive these payments. Provide evidence indicating three (3) years of continuance of these payments.

☐ Copy of driver's license and Social Security card, or passport. Copy of green card (front and back) for resident aliens

Documentation Required for a *Purchase* Application

The following documents must be submitted with your application if you are making a *new purchase*:

☐ Copy of fully executed agreement of sale for the property being purchased

☐ Real estate listing agreement or agreement of sale for your current home

Documentation Required for a *Refinance* Application

The following documents must be submitted with your application if you are *refinancing* a loan.

☐ Copy of deed for the property being refinanced

☐ The front page of homeowner's hazard insurance policy

11

Choosing
a Lender

"The use of money is all the advantage there is in having it."
– Benjamin Franklin

Choosing a Lender

There's a lot to understand about lenders, but the most important quality to look for is *honesty*. The amount of your monthly payment depends upon several variables, including whether or not you intend to occupy the property, how high your credit score is, what your debt-to-income ratio is, and how much your lender intends to profit from your loan.

Upside Up™ in Real Life

Dishonest Lenders

In 2003, I found out that our lender was cheating us. He'd tell us that our interest rate was locked, but would then wait for the market to drop further before actually locking our rate.

By gambling with our loan, he received a bonus called a "yield spread premium" for charging us a higher than market rate on our loans. We became suspicious when one of our refinance loans took more than 90 days to close.

Interest rates had gone *up* instead of *down*, and because he didn't lock our rate, we had to wait until the rates went back down to get the interest rate he'd told us he'd locked for us.

Another way dishonest loan officers can earn more money is to submit your loan as "owner-occupied" when you really don't intend to live in the property. This is *loan fraud* and you could go to jail!

If the loan documents are incorrect, don't sign them! Walk away from the closing and find an *honest* lender to help you finance your investments.

144

CHAPTER 11 - CHOOSING A LENDER

Each day, the lender receives a rate sheet showing the wholesale interest rate for each loan program. Lenders are paid by marking up the interest rate or by charging fees for origination, processing, and underwriting. Some lenders become greedy and charge both points and fees, which is why it's very important to find out how much your lender expects to make on your loan. I suggest looking them in the eye and asking them point blank, "How much do you intend to make on my loan?"

You don't need to do this with a real estate agent because the commission earned by the real estate agent is set by the seller when they list their home for sale. Because of fierce competition in the real estate business, the market dictates the amount of commission sellers are willing to pay.

The amount that a lender is paid is not as straight forward. The goal of many unscrupulous lenders is to charge as much as they possibly can without losing your business to a competing lender.

The easiest way a lender can increase their profit is to mark up the interest rate on your loan. They earn a bonus called a *yield spread premium* if they sell you a loan at a higher-than-market rate.

Let's assume that you have good credit, a low debt ratio, and intend to occupy the property. Suppose that your lender *could* give you a 7% interest rate on a loan amount of $200,000. If you tell them that you'd be happy with a loan of 7¾%, some will gladly initiate a loan at 7¾% and make thousands of dollars in the process.

For every one-eighth of one percent that a lender adds to the interest rate, they typically receive a bonus equal to one percent of the loan amount. On a $200,000 loan, one percent is equal to $2,000. The difference between a 7% interest rate and a rate of 7¾% is ¾%. Three-quarters could also be expressed as six-eighths.

On this loan, the lender would receive a yield spread premium of $12,000 in addition to any processing, origination, and other fees they may have already charged because they're paid one percent of the loan amount ($2,000) for every one-eighth of one percent higher they move your rate above the wholesale rate ($200,000 × 6 = $12,000).

This amount of commission is *excessive*; the national average earned by a loan officer is about $3,000 per loan. The extra ¾% interest on this $200,000 loan will add an extra $1,500 per year to your interest payment until the loan is paid off! This is why it's crucial to find an honest, relationship-based lender whom you can trust to act in your best interest.

Adding Risk Increases Your Rate

Sometimes when a lender increases the interest rate above the wholesale rate, it is not so they can make an additional profit. On the rate sheets that banks provide to their affiliates each day, there are added costs, called *hits*, for additional risks the borrower may bring with them. An explanation of some of these risks follows, as well as a sample penalty for each risk:

Non-owner occupied - Most homeowners will take better care of their property than tenants do. The banks know this, and they assess a penalty on loans in which the owner will not reside on the premises. **1 HIT**

Non-W-2 income - Lenders like to verify *everything!* Self-employed people don't have an employer that the lender can call to verify the amount of income they earn each month. There are no weekly or bi-weekly pay stubs to verify either. All the lender has is the income tax returns from previous years, which don't show whether the income came all at once or steadily each month. Because loan payments are made monthly, this introduces risk. **3 HITS**

Less than 20% down - When a borrower invests less than 20% of the purchase price as a down payment, the lender stands a greater risk of loss in the event they'll need to foreclose on the property. Because it takes six months or more to go through the foreclose process, several payments may be delinquent by the time the lender takes ownership. Then the lender must pay to market and sell the property. There is a good chance that a less-than-20% down payment from the buyer would not be enough to cover these expenses. **2 HITS**

Multi-family dwellings - Because there are fewer people in the market to buy a duplex, tri-plex, or other multi-family dwelling, lenders know that these properties might take longer to market in the event they would need to foreclose on them. Some banks treat a duplex the same as a single-family home, but charge higher rates and fees for three and four-unit properties. **3 HITS**

Before a lender can establish an interest rate for a loan, it must total the number of hits that the borrower has compiled. In the example above, I received one hit for not occupying the property, three hits for being self-employed, two hits for putting less than 20% down, and three hits for having a multi-family dwelling.

For each hit I receive, the lender will add ⅛% to my interest rate. The total number of hits I received in this example is nine, so the lender must add 1⅛% to my interest rate. If wholesale mortgage rate is at 7%, the lender will raise my rate to 8⅛% to cover the extra risks that I caused them to accept. The interest rate could go even higher if the loan officer adds their yield spread to the equation.

Niche Lenders

Some banks won't lend money on multi-unit properties such as a duplex, tri-plex, or multi-family apartments because their niche market is single-family residences (SFRs) with white picket fences in suburban neighborhoods.

Because SFRs appeal to a majority of the population, there is a much lower risk that the bank will lose money if they have to foreclose on the property and resell it. This is not the case with a 200-unit apartment building because there aren't a lot of people who would be able to afford such an expensive purchase.

If the lender had to foreclose on this type of investment, it might take a long time to sell and the lender might have to lower the price substantially in order to sell it. Lenders raise the interest rate and their fees to compensate for having to accept more risk.

Some financial institutions single out borrowers with very high credit scores as their niche. The risk of foreclosure is much lower with these people because they have a steady work history, pay their bills on time, and are not deeply in debt. Because their risk of loss is low, banks offer a much lower interest rate to borrowers who fall into this category.

Conversely, some lenders specialize in *subprime loans*. These loans are issued to people with very *low* credit scores. Borrowers who have extremely low credit scores don't have many choices about where they can borrow, so lenders are able to charge unusually high fees and substantially higher interest rates than most people would be willing to pay. It's a sort of "take it or leave it" situation for the borrowers in this category who want to achieve home ownership. This is the consequence of having a low credit score.

The higher rates and fees charged by lenders for these types of loans are necessary to compensate for the increased risk. Unfortunately, many of these borrowers will fail to repay the lender as promised and end up in foreclosure.

The risk of subprime loans going into default was significantly increased in the mid-2000s when lenders allowed buyers to obtain variable rate loans at low *teaser* rates, and then steadily increased their rates.

When a borrower's mortgage interest is at 4% one month and jumps to 6% the next, the mortgage payment is increased by 50% in one month! Because a home mortgage is the largest expense most people have, not many can absorb that kind of increase in their monthly budget.

Mortgage Banker or Mortgage Broker?

Lenders fall into two major groups: mortgage bankers and mortgage brokers. A mortgage banker works for a specific bank and can usually provide only the loan products that their employing bank has to offer. A mortgage broker has relationships with multiple banks and thus can offer a variety of loan programs.

Besides having a better selection of loan programs, another benefit of using a mortgage broker is that you'll know exactly how much money you're being charged on your loan. When a bank funds a loan internally, they're not required to disclose how much of a yield spread premium they're paying to the loan officer.

Because a mortgage *broker* is not an employee of the bank, the yield spread premium paid by the bank must be displayed on the HUD-1 closing statement to comply with the Real Estate Settlement Procedures Act (RESPA) that has governed real estate transactions in the United States since 1974.

The downside of using a mortgage broker is that there are sometimes higher fees because the mortgage broker is a "middle-man." My favorite lender (my wife) is a mortgage broker who uses a variety of banks depending on which loan product offers the best interest rate with the lowest fees.

If you buy only three-bedroom, two-bathroom, single-family homes with a down payment of 20%, you may be able to use your local bank or credit union's mortgage products. But when you deviate from single-family homes to duplexes and multi-unit structures, your local bank or credit union probably won't be the best choice for competitive rates.

I like to use a mortgage broker because of the variety of loan products they offer. If you have limited financing options, you may not be able to qualify for certain types of properties. You won't earn *any* money if you can't buy a property, so don't balk at paying slightly higher fees to someone who can get the deal done and close on time!

Good deals disappear fast in any market. If your lender has a history of not closing on time, you'll need to fire them and find someone who can follow through as promised. Be aware that the seller has no obligation to sell their property to you the day *after* the agreed upon closing date.

They can usually keep your earnest money and sell the property to the person in line behind you who's willing to pay more than you agreed to pay. This is a double win for the seller. Don't let it happen at your expense.

Many mortgage companies specialize in certain types of loans much like doctors specialize in a specific area of medicine. I recommend finding an experienced lender who specializes in working with *investors*. Lenders who specialize in investment lending will usually have a wider variety of loan programs than lenders who specialize mainly in financing primary residences.

It's important to get pre-qualified with someone who is experienced in investment lending so you'll know in advance how much you're qualified to borrow and thus, are able to spend.

Types of Loans

Although there are hundreds of loan programs available to purchase real estate, the two most common categories of loans are known as either *conventional* or *non-conventional* loans. Most lenders don't offer all of the loan programs available, so you'll have to shop for a lender who offers the loans that meet your investment needs.

Conventional Loans

Conventional loans are issued by private sector mortgage companies. In order to be bought or sold between banks, the loans must conform to a stringent set of standards that avoid excessive risk. Those who borrow more than 80% of the appraised value must purchase mortgage insurance to protect the lender much like the government does on VA and FHA loans (discussed later in this chapter).

In addition to mortgage insurance, conventional lenders require that borrowers have liquid assets remaining after closing. Lenders usually require cash reserves equal to a *minimum* of two months of principal, interest, property taxes, and hazard insurance. To further protect themselves, conventional lenders require that several months of property taxes and a year of hazard insurance are paid in advance by the borrower.

Unpaid hazard insurance will not protect the property from damage, and unpaid property taxes will result in a tax lien that takes precedence over the lender's mortgage. Either of these situations would introduce risk to the lender, so it requires the payments for these items to be made in advance.

To ensure that the hazard insurance and property tax payments are made in a timely manner, the lender maintains an escrow account that holds the payments you make in advance for insurance and taxes. When the tax and insurance bills come due, the lender pays them from this account.

Employment requirements - Conventional lenders have fairly strict requirements about a borrower's employment. The lender likes to see several years at the same job, because it shows stability. If you've recently changed jobs, it shouldn't be an issue, as long as your new job is in the same career field.

If I would have quit working at Raytheon and then started working in real estate, I would have had to show two years of income in real estate before I could qualify for a loan. Because I ran my real estate business concurrently while working at Raytheon, I had several years of tax returns showing real estate income, and thus was able to obtain loans without a problem after I left my job at Raytheon.

Bankers don't look favorably on lapses in employment because it shows instability. If you plan to take a few months off in between jobs, quit on the first day of one month and return to work by the last day of the next month. By planning your "time off," like this, your work history will show that your employment ended at your old job in one month and started at your new job the next month. You'll have gotten a 58 day sabbatical without an employment *gap* to worry about.

Bankers worry about employees who've reached the top of their earning potential and have no future advancement opportunities. In our fast-changing world, technologies can be obsolete in a few years.

Lenders prefer borrowers who are specialists in their career field because they have a high probability of continued employment. Employees with high levels of education and occupational training have a lower risk of being laid off, because employers are slow to discard their knowledge base.

If there is a layoff, highly skilled employees would be in much more demand than those with low or outdated skills. Low-skill employees face the biggest risk of lay off because they can be easily replaced.

Earnings ratios - To limit their risk even further, conventional lenders set basic guidelines for the amount of debt borrowers can carry. A borrower's debt-to-income ratio is calculated by dividing their total monthly debt payments by total monthly income.

The ratios are calculated two ways: The first ratio, called the *front-end ratio* calculates the percentage of the borrower's gross pay that the loan payment for their primary residence will consume.

The second ratio, called the *back-end ratio*, calculates the percentage of the borrower's gross pay that all of their recurring debt will consume. This includes credit cards, car payments, student loans, mortgages, and any other recurring payments. Table 11-1 shows the front-end and back-end ratios for various loans:

Table 11-1 Allowable Ratios for Conforming Loans

FIXED-RATE LOANS		
Loan-to-Value %	**Front-End Ratio**	**Back-End Ratio**
95%	28%	33%
90%	30%	36%
80%	33%	38%
ADJUSTABLE RATE LOANS		
Loan-to-Value %	**Front-End Ratio**	**Back-End Ratio**
ALL	28%	36%

According to the information in Table 11-1, if you earned $5,000 per month and were borrowing 80% of the appraised value of your home, your payment could not exceed 33% of your gross pay.

This equates to a maximum payment on your primary residence of $1,650 per month ($5,000 × 33% = $1,650). With a loan-to-value ratio of 80%, the total monthly payments on all of your recurring debt (back-end ratio) can not exceed 38%, which equates to $1,900 per month (utility bills aren't considered recurring debt).

Lenders allow investors to add, to the *Income* side of their loan application, 75% of the proposed rental income from the property being purchased. The amount of the mortgage on the property is added to the *Liabilities* side of the loan application.

If the monthly rent is 25% higher than the payment on the new loan, the rental property will have little or no effect on your front-end and back-end ratios. But, in order to qualify as an investor, you must show two years of previous landlord experience on your income tax returns.

Compensating Factors for High Loan Ratios

In the event your loan ratios are higher than those shown in Table 11-1, there are compensating factors that may allow for some leeway in the ratio guidelines. These compensating factors are as follows:

Large amount of cash reserves - If the balances in your bank accounts are enough to pay several months of mortgage payments, the chance of you defaulting on your loan is lessened significantly. The fact that you've been able to save several months worth of living expenses shows the lenders that you're a good money manager.

Minimal payment shock - If the new mortgage payment is not much more than your previous mortgage payment, there is less risk for *payment shock*. If you were previously living in your parent's basement rent-free and now want to take on a mortgage payment of $1,500, lenders will consider this to be a risk unless you can show that you've been saving a substantial amount of your income each month.

Liquid assets (able to repay loan) - If you have enough liquid assets (cash, securities, etc.) to pay off the loan you're applying for, the bank is not too worried about issuing a loan to you. Many retirees don't have a large monthly income but have enormous amounts of liquid assets.

Large cash down payment - If your down payment is a substantial portion of the purchase price, the bank will have little risk because the first money lost is yours. The lower the loan-to-value ratio, the safer the investment is for the lender.

Demonstrated ability to save and maintain good credit - Borrowers who have many assets and a strong credit score have proven themselves to have stable income and good money management skills. Lenders look very favorably on these behaviors because they demonstrate responsibility, which means less risk for the bank.

Likelihood of increasing earning capabilities - Lenders look favorably on borrowers who increase their value in the workplace. Employees who obtain advanced degrees are often rewarded with job promotions and pay increases. If you're approaching graduation, lenders often treat you as if you've already acquired the promotion and pay increase.

Very high credit score (720+) - In order to achieve a very high credit score, borrowers must have job stability, low debt-to-income ratios, and a solid history of paying their bills on time. Lenders believe that past behavior is a good indicator of future behavior and thus look very favorably on borrowers with very high credit scores.

Non-conventional Loans

These loans are also referred to as *non-conforming* loans because they don't conform to the standards required by the secondary loan markets where banks buy and sell loans from one another. Non-conventional loans fall into three categories: VA, FHA, and subprime.

VA loans - This loan program is overseen by the Veterans Administration. VA loans are only available to individuals who've served the United States in the armed forces. These loans allow veterans to obtain 100% financing on their home at an interest rate that is comparable to that received by non-veterans who pay a 20% down payment.

The interest rate for 100% financing is usually substantially higher because the risk to the issuing bank is much higher. The reason the banks aren't charging for higher risk is because they aren't experiencing higher risk. The U.S. government provides mortgage insurance on the top 20% of these loans, which means the lender's money is only at risk if the property value drops below 80% of the appraised value.

Unlike conventional appraisers, VA appraisers also act as home inspectors and may provide a list of repairs that must be completed before the loan will be approved. VA appraisers are notoriously conservative on their property valuation, which adds even more protection for the bank.

There are some closing costs that a buyer is not allowed to pay under this program, so a seller's closing costs will increase by several hundred dollars if the buyer is obtaining a VA loan. This can be a disadvantage to buyers in a strong seller's market because sellers may have other offers that don't face the risk of low appraisals and don't require these closing costs to be paid.

FHA loans - These loans are very similar to VA loans, but require the buyer to invest a down payment of 3% of the purchase price into the home. The U.S. government provides mortgage insurance on the top 17% of these loans, which means like VA loans, the lenders are only at risk if the property value drops below 80% of the appraised value.

FHA appraisals seem to be somewhat less conservative than VA appraisals, but still seem to come in on the low side of the range. Like a VA loan, there are some closing costs that a buyer is not allowed to pay, so the seller's closing costs usually increase by several hundred dollars for these types of loans.

Subprime loans - These loans are issued to people that present a higher than normal risk. The borrowers typically have either low credit scores, high debt-to-income ratios, or both. These risk factors may indicate that the borrowers do not have good money management skills or stable employment.

Either of these items could cause an inability to repay the loan, so these borrowers are turned away from mainstream lenders because they don't conform to the rigid guidelines required by conventional loan programs. The lenders who are willing to lend to these individuals charge much higher rates to compensate for the added risk. They often charge higher fees, stiff prepayment penalties, several points up front, and interest rates that are sometimes more than twice the rate that borrowers with good credit are able to obtain.

12

Understanding Your Market

"A market is the combined behavior of thousands of people responding to information, misinformation and whim."
– Kenneth Chang

Supply and Demand

In a free-market economy, the value of a property is the amount a buyer is willing to pay and the seller is willing to accept. This value changes as supply and demand change. When the supply of goods or services is scarce, demand is high; and when there is an abundant supply, demand is low.

In an *arms-length* transaction (between two unrelated parties), the value is established by the buyer and seller in the purchase agreement.

Two of the most significant factors driving demand for properties in any given area are school rankings and crime rates. Properties in areas with outstanding schools typically are in higher demand than those in areas with poorly ranked schools; properties in areas of low crime are preferred to those in areas of high crime. Published school scores and crime statistics are available in most communities, so check them out before making your purchase.

High demand typically results in a shortage. A *seller's market* develops because more people want to buy a home in an area than there are homes available. In this situation, homes sell very quickly and sellers can ask more for their home because there are fewer options for buyers who need a place to live.

In a seller's market, buyers are often forced to accept whatever properties are available—even properties in poor condition. It's not uncommon for sellers to receive multiple offers when demand is extremely high. If you're a buyer in a seller's market, you may have to offer more than the asking price—sometimes tens of thousands of dollars more—to ensure that your offer is accepted.

> ## *Upside Up™ in Real Life*
>
> ### <u>Buying in a Seller's Market</u>
>
> During the summer of 2005, there were only about 3,200 properties for sale in the Tucson real estate market. In a city of *one million people*, this created a tremendous inventory shortage. (Tucson is growing by about 2,000 persons per month.)
>
> One couple, trying to purchase a home during this time, generated six offers, each at least $10,000 *over* the asking price. None of their offers were accepted, even though we'd been searching the Multiple Listing Service every hour and making the offers on the first day the homes came on the market.
>
> Finally, on the Fourth of July, when most people were celebrating with their families, they got an offer accepted on a new listing by offering $16,000 over the asking price!
>
> A very strong seller's market can create unbelievably high demand. Situations like this don't typically last, but they present an ideal opportunity to sell your properties for incredible profits.

The tables turn, however, in a low-demand, *buyer's market,* when there is a surplus of homes available for sale relative to people who are purchasing homes. In this market, *buyers* are the scarce commodity and have the upper hand in determining the price.

When buyers have a large selection of homes to choose from, they choose the properties with the nicest views, upgrades, and amenities.

Properties with deferred maintenance, strange or unusual floor plans, or poor lot placement take a long time (sometimes years) to sell. If you're in a buyer's market, you should be able to negotiate a much lower price on these types of properties and ask the seller to pay your closing costs. Sellers are often willing to make concessions in slow markets.

Choosing a REALTOR®

By now you should have located a REALTOR® with whom you feel comfortable and whose judgment you trust. Nearly everyone has a friend or family member in the real estate business, but to obtain crucial information about your local real estate market, you'll need the help of a real estate professional who is experienced in selling the type of property you wish to purchase.

You probably wouldn't feel too comfortable letting a proctologist perform surgery on your knee because that is not their field of expertise. The same holds true for the real estate profession.

There are REALTORS® who specialize in relocating families. These agents can be very helpful before, during, and after your move to a new area. There are others who tend to sell properties in specific neighborhoods and are extremely knowledgeable about the schools, parks, and recreational activities in an area. Before you begin investing, you need to find someone who eats, drinks, and sleeps *investment* real estate.

If you needed surgery, you wouldn't want to be the first patient of a new doctor. You'd seek out the best surgeon you could find with the most experience in the relevant field of medicine. Why shouldn't the same be true for real estate investing?

CHAPTER 12 - UNDERSTANDING YOUR MARKET

You're about to make some of the most expensive investment decisions of your life. Wouldn't you want to find the most experienced investment property specialist available?

I recommend finding an agent who not only has experience selling investment properties, but also *owns* the type of rental properties you anticipate buying. You'll need to feel comfortable with them and know that their advice can be trusted. An inexperienced agent may be the most honest person in the world, but without experience and knowledge they will not be of much use to an investor.

Information empowers you to be able to make decisions based on facts, not beliefs. A REALTOR® has access to pertinent information about a property's history that cannot be obtained elsewhere.

For example, you can get a pretty good idea of the supply and demand for property in your area by looking at the average length of time it takes to sell a home and how closely homes are selling to their initial asking price. There are two statistics, known as "days on market" and "list-to-sale ratio," respectively, that provide that information. Both are available from your REALTOR®.

Days on Market

The time it takes to sell a home is referred to as the *days on market*. This statistic is useful to establish whether you're in a buyer's market or a seller's market. Days on market indicates the length of time that the property was actively for sale before an offer was accepted by the seller. In an extremely hot seller's market, it's not unusual to receive multiple offers on the first day a property is for sale.

When a market slows, the inventory of available homes will increase as markets change from having more buyers than sellers to having more sellers than buyers. When the number of buyers is shrinking and the number of sellers is growing, the time required to sell a home will increase steadily until the market changes its direction again.

Upside Up™ in Real Life

<u>New Jobs Increase Demand</u>

In October, 1998, Raytheon announced that they were closing their electronics manufacturing plant in Lewisville, Texas, and relocating the facility to Tucson, Arizona. My wife and I purchased a home a few weeks later while in Tucson on the first familiarization trip offered by the company.

By June 1999, more than 900 employees had relocated to Tucson from Texas. One of our co-workers who waited to purchase his home ended up paying $30,000 more than we'd paid for the exact floor plan. We'd viewed his home six months earlier, but opted against it due to several less-desirable characteristics: a west-facing back yard, a steep driveway, and close proximity to a busy road.

By purchasing our home shortly after the move was announced, we were able to acquire a superior property for a significantly lower price than those who waited to buy. We gained market appreciation driven in part by the higher demand of the other employees relocating to the area. Jobs have a lot to do with supply and demand in your local market, so pay attention to these sorts of changes.

If the number of days required to sell a home in one area is substantially higher than other areas you're considering, you might rethink whether you want to buy a home in the slower-moving location. You might face the same difficulty when you're ready to sell the property at a later date. Rural properties in outlying areas often take longer to sell because there is a lower demand for these homes due to the inconvenience of driving long distances every day.

Before buying, try to assess the economic stability of an area, such as whether a nearby plant or military base might be closing soon. Such changes could lead to decreased demand for property in the area and probably to reduced values. If you can establish a reason for such slow downs or closures, you'll have a better idea of whether there will be a long-term effect on the value of property in the area.

Conversely, if a new plant or facility is being built near the property you are interested in, there's a good chance that the demand for homes in the area will increase, along with the property's value. This is why it's important to do the best you can to try to determine the economic factors that might affect your property's future value.

List-to-Sell Ratio

The *list-to-sale ratio* can also help you determine how "hot" a real estate market is by comparing the asking price to the selling price of recent transactions. In the event that the reports from your REALTOR® don't provide the data as a percentage, you can divide the selling price by the asking price to get the ratio.

For example, if the asking price of a property was $250,000 and it sold for $238,000, you would divide the selling price of $238,000 by the asking price of $250,000 to find the list-to-sale ratio of 95.2%. To get the average list-to-sale ratio for the area, you'd calculate the list-to-sale ratio for each of the recent sales in the area and then average them.

An average list-to-sale ratio of 95.2% (calculated above) indicates that there are more homes for sale than there are buyers to purchase them. We know this because on average, sellers had to lower their price by nearly five percent in order to sell their homes.

Due to the abundant supply of homes on the market, the sellers may be willing to negotiate on their price. This often depends upon how motivated they are, and how their asking price compares to that of similar homes.

If the sellers have already purchased another home, they may be very motivated to sell because they're making two mortgage payments each month. Most families have not budgeted for two mortgage payments and thus cannot afford to pay for an empty home for long periods of time.

If the average list-to-sale ratio is over 100%, you'll know that the real estate market is very competitive, with most homes selling for more than the asking price. The list-to-sale ratio is an indicator, not a bible. A seller's ability or willingness to negotiate will depend on their individual situation, how urgently they need to sell, and whether they priced their home at the low end or the high end of the price range in which other homes have been sold.

List-to-sale ratios can vary widely, depending upon such factors as the local economy, exclusivity of the subdivision, price range, and school district. An experienced REALTOR® can provide a lot of insight on why some properties sell for much higher prices than others. If your real estate agent doesn't know what a list-to-sale ratio is, you should find a different agent!

Signs of a Motivated Seller

Vacant homes, divorce sales, and frequent (or large) price reductions are good indications that a seller is motivated. A vacant home is usually a dead giveaway that the sellers have moved on with their lives and are anxious to sell their former home. Although a vacant home is easier to show, it doesn't show as well as a furnished home.

A divorce sale can usually be spotted a mile away because the home has only half the furniture that was once present and the closets have only one spouse's clothing. Since some sellers are single (i.e., not divorcing) and might not own a lot of furniture, look for depression marks in the carpet that indicate furniture was once present but is now missing.

Another good indication of a seller's motivation is the frequency (how close together) and the amount of their price reductions. Those who are in no hurry to sell usually space their price reductions at least three weeks or more apart. Weekly price changes usually indicate that a seller is desperate.

All price reductions suggest that the sellers are starting to question the value of their property. Owners of homes that have been on the market a long time are usually more prone to accept offers for less than their asking price. But, many times, homeowners are reluctant to lower their price in the first week or two because they don't feel the market value of their home has been *tested*.

Showing Activity

A good way to tell how much showing activity a property has received is to make note of the number of names on the sign-in sheet when you visit the property. Compare the number of names on the sign-in sheet to the number of days the property has been on the market to find the number of visits per day or week.

Property History

Ask your REALTOR® to check the history of the property on the Multiple Listing Service (MLS). This information may show when the sellers bought it, how much they paid, and how long it's been for sale.

Numbers sometimes lie, but history doesn't! Be on the lookout for a false read! The number of days on market shown on the listing doesn't always tell the complete story. It's common in the real estate industry to cancel a listing when it doesn't sell after a certain period, and then to re-list the property. In some areas, when a new listing is started the number of days on market is reset to *zero*.

This isn't intentional trickery. After a home has been for sale for a long time, buyers might get the impression that there is something wrong with the property, but this often is not the case. For instance, the sellers might have received a contract during the first week the home was for sale, but the buyers were unable to close after having the home in escrow for several months. When the home goes back on the market, it will appear as if it's been for sale for two months, which could imply that it has problems or is overpriced.

Sometimes the sellers ask to start a new listing to generate more interest after they've reduced the price substantially.

Checking the listing history of a property will show how many times the property has been listed for sale in recent years.

The history can also indicate how many offers might have been tendered and fallen through since the property was listed. This information can reveal crucial insight about the seller, including how frequently they've reduced the price and how desperate they are to sell.

Selling a home is an emotional roller coaster. The best time to make an offer is immediately after another offer is cancelled. When the sellers have just gone from the highest point (thinking their home was sold) to the lowest point (knowing they have to start all over again) they are often willing to accept a lower offer than the one that just fell through to recover the "high" of knowing that their home is sold and they can move on with their lives.

Asking Price

To sell an imperfect property in a buyer's market, sellers must lower their price to compete with the nicer homes. As more and more properties become available for sale, sellers who have an urgent need to sell will continue to lower their price until their property is sold. As these properties sell at lower and lower prices, they begin to drive the value lower for other properties in the area.

In a seller's market, the demand for housing can create bidding wars for above average properties because there are more buyers in search of these homes than there are homes in this condition. After these sales are recorded, the comps for other homes are affected favorably because of the high prices that the bidding wars produced.

Many sellers have an emotional attachment to their home. They believe that their home is worth more than anyone else's, so they insist on listing their home even higher than the price produced by the bidding war. If the market is extremely hot, and the house really is a high-end property, another bidding war may ensue that drives the value even higher.

An overpriced home will not sell in any market until the price is adjusted to meet or beat the prices of competing properties. Buyers really don't care how much the seller *needs* out of a property or why they need it. The market sets the price and is oblivious to the needs of the seller.

13

Establishing Value

"I conceive that the great part of the miseries of mankind are brought upon them by false estimates they have made of the value of things." – Benjamin Franklin

Appraisals

Before you write an offer on a property, you'll need to establish the fair market value. This can be accomplished by hiring a certified real estate appraiser. Many people think that appraising a home is an exact science that automatically establishes the absolute value of a property, but this isn't true.

An appraisal is one person's *opinion* of how much the property might sell for. Because there are aggressive appraisers and conservative appraisers, the appraised value can vary widely. I've seen appraisals on the same property vary by as much as ten percent! The market value (what a buyer is willing to pay) may be much different than the appraised value, depending upon how badly a buyer wants the property or how desperate the seller is.

Banks hire an appraiser to verify that the price being paid for the property is reasonable for the area, based on the sales of other similar properties.

To prove to the bank that the property is worth as much as the buyer is paying, the appraiser must provide the addresses and pictures of several other properties recently sold in the immediate area. The value of a single family home is usually dependent on the price that other single family homes have been sold for in the area.

The properties being compared must be of a similar size and type. Adjustments to account for amenities such as granite counter tops, tile floors, garages, and swimming pools are made by adding or subtracting from the value of the home being appraised.

Now that you know there's not an exact scientific formula to establish the value of a property, you may want to get information easier, faster, and cheaper for your *initial* review.

CHAPTER 13 - ESTABLISHING VALUE

Your REALTOR® can provide a trend analysis and a comparative market analysis

Trend Analysis

A trend analysis shows the average price per square foot that a neighborhood has sold for during the past several years. I like to run a report for each of the last five years to establish the long-term appreciation history of the neighborhood. I usually stay within a quarter mile of the property that I'm considering.

Past appreciation is no guarantee that a property will appreciate in the future, but the information provides a much longer-term look at the neighborhood than a comparative market analysis showing only the data from recent sales.

Long-term appreciation is an important component of real estate investing, even if you don't include it in your profit projections. If property values in the area have stagnated or are heading in a downward direction, you should re-think whether you still wish to buy the property.

Comparative Market Analysis

Commonly referred to as a *comp* or *CMA*, the comparative market analysis helps to establish the demand, availability, and price of similar properties on the market in the surrounding area. A good comp comprises three parts:

1) a list of the other homes *currently for sale* in the area

2) a list of area homes that are *under contract* to be sold

3) a list of homes that have recently *sold* in the area

The accuracy of the comparison is dependent upon how recently the other sales were completed and how similar in terms of features and location the other properties are to the one you're trying to evaluate.

You should perform a CMA using homes within one-quarter mile (or one-half mile, if necessary) from the property you are evaluating, depending on the number of homes for sale in the neighborhood.

Compare the list of homes that are currently for sale in that area to the list of homes that have sold in the last six months (if prices are fluctuating, you may want to limit your search to the past *three* months).

For example, if seventy-two homes were sold in the previous six months, you can easily establish that twelve homes are sold on average each month. If the number of homes actively listed for sale is one-hundred-and-twenty, there's a ten-month supply of homes on the market. (120 homes ÷ 12 homes sold per month = 10 month supply).

This indicates that it's a buyer's market (more supply than demand) and you can probably negotiate on the price. If there are only 24 homes actively for sale (a two month supply), this indicates that you're in a seller's market (more demand for homes than homes for sale). In this situation, you may need to offer the full asking price in order to have your offer accepted.

I recommend a sample size of 5 – 9 properties for each part of the CMA (for sale, under contract, and sold). If a comp doesn't produce an adequate sample size you have two choices. You can either go farther back in time or choose a wider market area. If prices have remained stable for the past year, you can change the default from the past six months to the past twelve months, but if prices have been changing rapidly, you won't want to go back any further.

If you widen the search area from one-quarter mile to one-half mile, you should be able to substantially increase the sample size, but you may need to keep the comps in the same subdivision if there is a gated community, luxury home neighborhood, or starter home neighborhood nearby.

Analyzing the MLS Data

To establish the value of a property, you'll need to review the following *MLS data* (from the Multiple Listing Service) for the surrounding area:

SOLD listings
ACTIVE listings
ACTIVE CONTINGENT listings
ACTIVE CAPA listings
PENDING listings

SOLD listings – When analyzing market data, you should always look at the properties that have been *sold*. This is the most accurate data available because these are transactions that have been completed, or *closed*. You can learn a lot about market conditions from closed transactions because they reveal the price a buyer offered and a seller accepted for each property. If these transactions were between unrelated parties, then *market value* has been established. Be aware, though, that comparing properties to one another is never exact because no two properties are exactly the same.

ACTIVE listings – You should also analyze competing properties that are for sale, or *Active*, in the area's market. This helps to establish how many properties similar to yours are for sale.

Active listings are extremely valuable in helping sellers find the right price for their property. When the data suggests that my seller's price expectation is too high, I load them into my car and we visit the other properties listed for sale that potential buyers would compare to their home. There's nothing more convincing than a nicer home being offered at a lower price to reset a seller's expectation of what their home is worth.

If there is a huge mismatch between the cost per square foot of *Active* listings and *Sold* listings, the price per square foot of properties under contract may be useful to fill in the blanks. This is why I review *Active Contingent*, *Active Capa*, and *Pending* listings (see below).

Although you won't know the price details of the contract until after the property closes, you'll know that the asking price attracted an offer. Using the list-to-sale ratio, we can get an estimate of what the property will sell for by multiplying the asking price by the ratio other homes have sold for in relation to their asking price.

In some cases, even in a slow market, you could ask more than the comps would suggest—and get it from a buyer. For instance, if you lived in an area where smaller homes were in demand and you happened to have one of the few smaller homes available, buyers might pay a premium for such a home.

ACTIVE CONTINGENT listings –Properties that are listed as *Active Contingent* indicate that the sellers have accepted a contract from a buyer, but the contract is contingent upon an acceptable home inspection, appraisal, and the buyer obtaining a loan. During the inspection phase of the contract, the potential buyers are busily completing their due diligence.

The buyers change the terms of the contract when they come back with a repair list after their inspections have been completed. If the seller is unwilling or unable to repair all of the items the buyer requests, the buyer has the right to cancel the contract. When the buyer and seller have a "meeting of the minds" regarding any repairs to be completed (and by whom), the contract status is changed to *Pending*.

ACTIVE CAPA listings – These properties have an accepted offer, but with a specific condition, or contingency (usually, the buyer needs to sell their home before they can purchase the new one). In these contracts, the sellers typically reserve the right to accept offers from other buyers who don't have any such conditions. (*CAPA* stands for "can accept purchase agreement.")

In the event an offer without a contingency is received from another buyer, the seller must give the original buyers the opportunity to remove the condition. If after a specific period (usually 72 hours), the original buyers are unwilling or unable to remove the contingency, the seller can cancel the first contract and accept the offer from the buyers who don't need to sell their home.

Upside Up™ in Real Life

Generate a Backup Offer

In 2005, we needed to move our real estate business from our home to a commercial office building. We decided on a new office park on a major thoroughfare within three miles of our home.

We wanted to purchase a $310,000 lot adjacent to the major traffic corridor because it would provide free advertising to the thousands of vehicles passing by every day. After finding that the lot was already under contract, we opted to purchase a much smaller lot at the rear of the office park for $102,000.

Because we *really* wanted the exposure of the front lot, we put a clause in our contract on the rear lot that gave us the first right of refusal in the event the other buyer fell out. Several months later, the other buyer cancelled their contract on the front lot and we were able to purchase the property.

We opted to build on the back lot first, so the front lot remained vacant. Just as a major road-widening project was nearing completion, we were offered $500,000 for the front property. We turned down the offer, but a few months later were offered $600,000. We ended up settling for $620,000, twice what we'd paid after holding the property for less than two years!

On a desirable property, I recommend that you generate a back-up offer. Just because someone else has an accepted contract doesn't mean that they'll follow through; deals are cancelled every day. A back-up position *guarantees* that you're the next in line!

PENDING listings – On properties that are listed as *Pending,* the buyer and seller are usually past the inspection period and have agreed to which repairs, if any, will be completed prior to closing. The parties are progressing toward closing, with the buyer's lender and the title company preparing all the necessary closing documents.

The number of pending listings is a reliable indicator of how many properties will sell in the next thirty days. This information can help you determine in advance if a market is slowing down or heating up.

Price per Square Foot

A fairly accurate indication of a home's value can be obtained by using the price per square foot paid by other families in the neighborhood. This is done by dividing the sale price of a home by its size (square feet of living space). This information is available either from the MLS (Sold listings) or from the County Assessor's office.

As an example, if a 1,000-square–foot home sold for $200,000, you would divide $200,000 by 1,000 to find that the home was sold at $200 per sq. ft. ($200,000 ÷ 1,000 sq. ft. = $200/sq. ft.).

You'll also need to be aware of construction type, age, quality, and condition of the property, so you don't compare masonry homes with frame homes, old homes with new homes, custom homes with tract homes, or perfectly maintained homes with run-down shacks. Other amenities to consider when evaluating a home's value per square foot are central air conditioning, multiple garage stalls, swimming pools, patios, views, and orientation (in Arizona, a west-facing back yard is undesirable due to the heat from the afternoon sun).

Adjusting for Age and Lot Size

Sometimes adjustments are required to account for age, square footage, and lot size. If one property has substantially more land than another, it will usually sell for a higher price. Many real estate agents use the price per square foot to compare properties to one another. They'll get an artificially high price per square foot on properties with excess acreage and will need to make an adjustment for the extra land.

The same effect can often be found when there is a substantial difference in the age of homes. The high price per square foot of the superior properties cannot be transferred to properties that don't have the preferable age, acreage, or amenities, but many sellers try.

Lot Premiums

Home builders long ago figured out that they could ask a lot more for a home on a hilltop than they could for one in a hole. The hilltop home has more desirable views and privacy than the home at the bottom of the hill, thus the more desirable home will *always* sell first.

The cost to build either home is the same, so builders adjust the cost of the land by applying a "lot premium" on their more desirable lots. This makes the less desirable lots appear to be a good deal to buyers who cannot afford the premium lots.

Many builders won't allow *all* of the premium lots to be sold until the subdivision is sold out. Otherwise they'd have only the undesirable lots left to sell as they phased out the subdivision. If there are no higher priced lots for sale, the lower priced lots wouldn't seem like a good deal, and thus would be harder to sell.

Upside Up™ in Real Life

<u>Wait for a Better Lot</u>

In 2002, I was at a new home subdivision with one of my clients. The builder was releasing lots in phases, and all of the desirable lots in the current phase had been sold. My clients were nearly persuaded to accept a less desirable lot, but I advised them to walk away.

We didn't make it to the car before the sales person came running out after us telling us that he could contact his supervisor and get them to release the next phase. Because of holding firm to what they wanted, my clients were able to get first choice of the lots available in the next phase rather than next-to-last-choice in an already picked over section of lots.

<u>Adjusting for Home Size</u>

Square footage is another anomaly to be aware of when comparing properties. The value of a home includes both fixed costs and variable costs. Fixed costs include the cost of the land, the cost to run electricity, natural gas, water, sewer, cable, and telephone lines, as well as hookups for kitchen and laundry appliances (most homes only have one kitchen and one laundry room). Variable costs are all the costs that increase as the size of the home increases. These costs include concrete, lumber, insulation, sheetrock, exterior sheathing, paint, and trim.

If a 1,000-square-foot home is built on the property, the fixed costs are divided by 1,000 square feet to establish the cost per square foot of the fixed costs.

If a 2,000-square-foot home is constructed on the same lot, the fixed costs remain the same, because the land cost is the same, the utility runs are the same, and the cost to connect kitchen and laundry appliances is the same. Because this home is twice as large as the 1,000-square-foot home, the fixed costs are divided over twice the area, which makes them account for only *half* as much of the overall value.

For example, if the fixed costs are $35,000 for both houses, they would be $35 per square foot for the 1,000-square-foot home, and $17.50 per square foot for the 2,000-square-foot home.

The cost to buy a larger home is nearly always going to be less per square foot than the cost to buy a smaller home. You'll find this to be true everywhere, from new home construction to neighborhoods with 100-year-old homes.

This is why it's important to find homes of similar size for your comparisons. If you build a large home in a small home neighborhood, you won't be able to sell the home for the same price per square foot as the smaller homes. When comparing properties, I recommend that you try to stay within +/- 200 square feet of the home that you're attempting to evaluate, if possible.

Adjusting for Added Features

Buyers may be willing to pay more for added features, such as pools, garages, and air conditioning, and also for upgrades, such as granite countertops, ceramic tile flooring, and fireplaces. Use caution before *assuming* you'll receive more for these items. Research should be completed prior to buying a home to determine which features add value in a particular area. An appraiser is the best source for this information.

If, for example, you add a three-stall garage in a neighborhood where none of the other homes have any garages, you probably won't be able to recover the cost of constructing the garage.

The same holds true for installing granite countertops in a mobile home. I'm sure the new owners would love them, but they probably won't be willing to pay as much as they cost.

Analyzing Rental Properties

Rental properties are purchased for different reasons than single-family homes and, thus, need to be analyzed differently. The reason that single-family homes can't be accurately compared to a multi-family property is because the intended use is different. Families buy homes to live in and investors buy homes to produce income.

Most families wouldn't purchase a multi-family dwelling to live in because this type of property doesn't fit their needs. (Parents of teen-aged children might fantasize about having a separate building for their kids, but few go through with it.)

To establish an accurate value, rental properties must be compared to other rental properties and single-family homes must be compared to other single-family homes.

Where you live is a personal choice that involves a lot of emotion. When buying their personal homes, even investors base their decision on emotion. But when buying an investment property, you will need to use logic and keep emotion out of the equation.

The amount that the neighbors paid for their property is of little concern to an investor. Investors mostly care about how much income the property will produce. Good investors put their money where it will produce the highest income.

There are three indicators that allow investors to quickly compare dissimilar properties to one another:

1) Gross Rent Multiplier (GRM)

2) One-percent Rule

3) Capitalization Rate

Gross Rent Multiplier

The *Gross Rent Multiplier (GRM)* is a simple equation that divides the purchase price by the total rent to determine the length of time it takes for the rent to equal the purchase price. The length of time can be presented in years or in months, but either way, this tool is a very fast way to determine whether or not a property has the potential to make a profit.

Higher rent properties usually sell for higher prices than lower rent properties because investors are willing to pay a higher price for a larger income stream.

When using the GRM to evaluate a property, remember that expenses are not included (i.e., not deducted from the total rent received) in the calculation. Two properties may have identical rents, but one property owner may pay all the utilities and the other doesn't. This can drastically affect your return and is why GRM should only be used to determine whether a property has the *potential* for profit.

One-percent Rule

Another quick way to check the propensity for profit is the *One-percent Rule*. This version of analysis is popular because it doesn't involve any mathematical equations and can be accomplished with only your *thumb*. If you pick up a listing sheet and place your thumb over the last two zeros of the asking price, you'll be looking at *one percent* of the total.

The monthly rent produced by the property should be close to one percent of the purchase price if the property is going to produce a positive cash flow.

For example, if a property is listed for $240,000 and you cover the two right-most digits with your thumb, you'll see $2,400. This suggests that the property needs to rent for about $2,400 per month to have a profitable cash flow.

If you have a lot of listings to analyze, there is no quicker way to weed through the stack than the One-percent Rule. It allows you to quickly establish whether the property has the *propensity* to earn money. Please note that the One-percent Rule works best at interest rates of 10%.

If the interest rate of your loan is less than 10%, lower rents may be acceptable because the monthly interest expense is lower. Like the gross rent multiplier, the One-percent Rule is a *gauge*, not a bible. It might appropriately be called the "rule of thumb"!

Capitalization Rate

The gross rent multiplier and the One-percent Rule are quick ways to establish whether or not to spend a lot of time analyzing a property. Because neither of these indicators takes into account the expenses of a property, they cannot determine the profitability, only the *potential* for profit.

The *Capitalization Rate* (commonly referred to as *cap rate* or *cap*) takes vacancy and expenses into account and provides the investor with the rate of return the investment would produce if there was no debt.

For example, a property with a cap rate of .06 earns 6% of the purchase price each year after vacancy loss and expenses are subtracted. In other words, the property earns $6 per year for every $100 invested. Compared to the interest paid on checking accounts, this looks pretty good!

The cap rate doesn't include the benefit received from income tax refunds, so your rate of return after taxes may improve, depending on your tax bracket and the amount of debt service you pay on the property.

14

Writing
an Offer

"Don't be afraid to take a big step. You can't cross a chasm in two small jumps."– David Lloyd George

Writing an Offer

Your REALTOR® can assist you in locating the data outlined in the previous two chapters. This data and a good understanding of the current market conditions in the area will help you establish the amount to offer on the property you're considering.

When all of the data has been gathered and analyzed, you'll need to decide whether or not to make an offer on the property. As an investor, the number of properties you're able to buy is limited by the amount of money you have available for down payments.

A few simple changes in your buying strategy will help to substantially reduce the amount of cash you'll need to purchase a property. These money saving strategies will help you accelerate the frequency of your purchases, and will allow you to purchase *three* properties with less money than is typically required to purchase only *two*.

A Typical Offer

Let's assume that you establish the value of a duplex to be $200,000. Using the method most investors have been trained to follow, you would write an offer for $200,000 with a 10% down payment of $20,000. The remaining $180,000 of the purchase price would be borrowed from a bank or other lending institution.

The closing costs typically would cost about two percent of the loan amount, depending upon whether or not the lender charges an origination fee. If an origination fee (usually one percent) is charged by the lender, your closing costs will be that much higher.

Let's assume that there *is* an origination fee, so we'll estimate that your closing costs are 3% of the loan amount, which is equal to $5,400 ($180,000 × .03 = $5,400).

Let's further assume that while viewing this property, you found that about $2,000 in repairs are needed to correct an unsafe condition. If the seller refuses to complete the repairs and you decide to go forward with transaction anyway, you'll need to spend the $2,000 immediately after closing to reduce your liability.

Let's assume that the property is currently rented, and the seller is holding a security deposit of $2,000 (one month's rent) from the tenants. This money will be transferred to you when you buy the property, but won't need to be refunded to the tenants until they move out.

Someday, you'll need to either refund the money to the tenants or spend it to repair damages, but unless prohibited by the laws in your state, you can use the deposit money to reduce the amount of cash you must bring to the closing table.

Some states may require that the money be placed in a separate interest-bearing account, but in Arizona, this is not the case. I can use the tenant's deposits to further reduce the amount I'll need to bring to closing.

The amount of cash you'll need for this purchase is calculated by adding the down payment, closing costs, and initial repair costs. If allowed by your state, you can subtract the amount of the security deposit. The equation for this would be: $20,000 down payment + $5,400 closing costs + $2,000 repairs - $2,000 security deposit (if local laws allow) = $25,400 cash to close. This transaction is presented in Table 14-1.

Table 14-1 Typical Offer

Typical Offer	
Sales Price	$200,000
Cash Required	
Down Payment	$ 20,000
Closing Costs	$ 5,400
Repairs	$ 2,000
Rents	$ 0
Security Deposit	($ 2,000)
Total Required to Close	**$ 25,400**

The Cash Preservation Offer

I like to write offers that minimize the amount of cash I must invest in each property. In this scenario, instead of paying the asking price of $200,000 (as I might normally do), my offer to the seller would be $207,400. That should get their attention!

To ensure that the seller won't have to pay a higher real estate commission due to the higher sales price, we calculate the real estate commission on a sales price of $200,000.

To make my offer stronger, I could increase the earnest money to 2% or more of the offer price. This gesture would show that I'm serious about my intent to purchase their property. I'll offer a down payment of 10% as in the previous example, but because the purchase price is now higher, the down payment will have to be higher too. Ten percent of the $207,400 purchase price makes the down payment $20,740.

Because I'm paying the seller $7,400 more than their asking price for their property, I'm going to ask them to pay $5,400 toward my closing costs and $2,000 for the required repairs. This won't cost the seller anything because both of these costs are paid at the closing table with the additional money the seller receives from me.

This strategy is attractive to sellers because they don't have to come out-of-pocket with any cash in order to sell their property to me. Sellers *always* take the path of least resistance, and I'm making it very easy on them by giving them the money to pay for my closing costs and repairs.

Table 14-2 Cash Preservation Offer

Cash Preservation Offer	
Sales Price	$207,400
Cash Required	
Down Payment	$ 20,740
Closing Costs	$ 0
Repairs	$ 0
Rents	$ 0
Security Deposit	($ 2,000)
Total Required to Close	**$ 18,740**
YOU SAVE (compared to Typical Offer)	**$ 6,660**

By writing the offer strategically, the same fees are being paid, but because I increased the purchase price and asked the seller to pay the closing costs and repairs for me, my out-of-pocket expense is only the $20,740 for the down payment.

If I'm able to use the security deposit at closing, the amount I need to close will be reduced from $25,400 to $18,740, a savings of $6,660. A summary of this offer can be found in Table 14-2.

You can further reduce the amount of cash needed to close by strategically setting the closing date. Many buyers and sellers like to close on the last day of the month to avoid paying another rent or mortgage payment. I don't think this is a good idea.

Escrow companies are busy closing everyone else at the end of the month, which means they have less time to verify the accuracy of my transaction. I'd much rather reschedule than get a "rush job" on an investment worth hundreds of thousands of dollars. Your escrow officer will appreciate you for moving the closing away from the end of the month.

When purchasing an investment property, I don't want to scramble on the day after closing to track down the tenants or collect the rent. For properties that are already rented, I like to close the day *after* the rents are collected.

Because I review the leases during the inspection period, I know when the rents are due. If the leases start on the first day of the month, I usually set my closing date for the second day of the month. If the leases don't start on the first day of the month, I set the closing date for the day after the rents are due.

By closing the day *after* the rents are collected, I'm making the seller responsible for collecting the rents for the next month. This is much better than attempting to collect rents from people you may have never met on the day after you've purchased a property.

The extra month gives me time to establish a rapport with the tenants and prepare a new lease for them to sign (if they're not on a term lease). From a financial perspective, this strategy reduces even further the amount of cash I need at closing because the rent collected for the month is prorated.

When I close on the second day of the month, the seller will have owned the property for one day during the month and I will own it the remaining 30 days. Let's assume that the rent is $2,000 per month (this is what the One-percent Rule suggests the rent will be when the purchase price is $200,000).

Assuming that we're purchasing the property in a 31-day month, the escrow company will prorate the rent by dividing the total rent of $2,000 by the number of days in the month to arrive at the rental fee per day ($2,000 ÷ 31 days = $64.52/day).

At the closing table, the escrow officer will charge the seller for the remaining rent of $1935.48 and give a credit to me! This lowers the amount of cash needed for closing by another $1,935, bringing the total amount to $16,805 ($28,740 - $1,935 = $16,805).

At the time you purchase a property, the escrow officer collects mortgage interest through the end of the current month. After that, mortgage interest is paid the month *after* it accrues. For example, the interest accrued in July would be paid in your August 1 mortgage payment.

If you close on July 31, you'd pay one day of interest at the closing table for July, and your first mortgage payment would not be due until the September 1. The August payment isn't due because interest accrued in August is paid in your September payment.

If instead of closing on July 31, you closed on August 2, the rent would be pro-rated by the escrow company and you'd receive a credit for 30 days of the rent.

Mortgage interest would also be pro-rated, and you'd be charged for 30 days of interest for August on the day of closing. Because the August interest is paid at closing, a September payment is not required, thus your first payment on this property would not be due until October 1!

Using this approach, you'll pay more interest at closing, but the rent credit will more than offset the interest. Because your first payment is not due for two months, you'll be able to collect rent *twice* before making your first mortgage payment! A summary of both the typical and cash preservation offers can be found in Table 14-3.

Table 14-3 Typical and Cash Preservation Offers

Typical Offer		Cash Preservation Offer	
Sales Price	$200,000	Sales Price	$207,400
Cash Required		**Cash Required**	
Down Payment	$ 20,000	Down Payment	$ 20,740
Closing Costs	$ 5,400	Closing Costs	$ 0
Repairs	$ 2,000	Repairs	$ 0
Rents	$ 0	Rents	$(1,935)
Deposits	$(2,000)	Deposits	$(2,000)
Cash to Close	$ 25,400	**Cash to Close**	$ 16,805
		YOU SAVE	$ 8,595

Offer Comparison

Because the buyer with a typically written contract closed at the end of the month, they will not receive any prorated rents from the seller at closing, but will save on prepaid mortgage interest to the bank for the first month.

The Cash Preservation method of writing the contract substantially reduces the $25,400 we'd have to spend if we closed on the first of the month using a typical offer.

This comparison is illustrated in Table 14-4.

Table 14-4 THREE homes for less money than TWO!

Typical Offer		Cash Preservation Offer	
Sales Price	$200,000	Sales Price	$207,400
Cash Required		**Cash Required**	
Down Payment	$ 20,000	Down Payment	$ 20,740
Closing Costs	$ 5,400	Closing Costs	$ 0
Repairs	$ 2,000	Repairs	$ 0
Rents	$ 0	Rents	$ (1,935)
Deposits	$ (2,000)	Deposits	$ (2,000)
Cash to Close	$ 25,400	**Cash to Close**	$ 16,805
YOU SAVE	$ 0	**YOU SAVE**	$ 8,595
Money Needed for **TWO** Rental Homes	$ 50,800	Money Needed for **THREE** Rental Homes	$ 50,415

The difference is a whopping $8,595 ($25,400 - $16,805 = $8,595), a savings of 33.8%. If you were able to save this much on each purchase using the Cash Preservation Offer, you could buy *three* properties with less cash than you'd need to buy *two* properties using a Typical Offer!

Are my payments slightly higher because I borrowed more money? Yes! Every additional $1,000 borrowed at 7% interest causes my payment on a 30 year loan to increase by $6.65 per month.

I've borrowed $186,660 ($207,400 purchase price - $20,740 down payment = $186,660) and the loan amount on the typically written contract was $180,000 ($200,000 - $20,000 = $180,000), so my mortgage amount is $6,660 more than the typically written contract would have been.

The additional $6,660 in debt will make my interest payment $44.31 higher each month. Interest is deductible on your income tax, so assuming that I fall in the 28% tax bracket, I'll receive 28% of the interest back in tax savings, which equals $12.41 ($44.31 × .28 = $12.41). This brings the difference to only $31.90 per month ($44.31 - $12.41 = $31.90).

It will take more than *seventeen years* of paying the extra $31.90 per month to reach the $6,660 that I would have paid at the closing table. By then I will probably have either sold the property or refinanced it several times.

To compare the rate of return I receive using the Cash Preservation method to the rate of return other investors will receive using the Typical approach, let's assume that this property earns $200 per month in positive cash flow after all expenses have been paid.

Those using the Typical method would accumulate a positive cash flow of $2,400 ($200 per month × 12 months =

$2,400). Because they invested $25,400 and produced a $2,400 income for the year, the cash-on-cash return is 9.44% ($2,400 ÷ $25,400 = .0944).

My cash flow will not be as high as the other investor's because my mortgage payment is $31.90 higher each month. This makes my monthly cash flow $168.10 ($200.00 - $31.90 = $168.10) and my annual cash flow $2,017 ($168.10 × 12 = $2,017.20).

To calculate my cash-on-cash return, I divide the annual cash flow of $2,017 by the total out-of-pocket investment of $16,805 to find that my cash-on-cash return is 12.00% ($2,017 ÷ $16,805 = .1200).

Using the Cash Preservation method produced a rate of return 21.3% higher than the typical investor's return, and I invested 33% less money!

In the event real estate in the area appreciates (though, remember, I never depend on it!), my profit will be significantly higher than the other investor's profit because I'll own *three* properties for every *two* that they were able to purchase!

Playing "Hot Potato" with the Keys

Interest for the first month of the loan is paid at the closing table, so the first payment is not due until the beginning of the *second* month. When a rental property is initially purchased, you have a unique opportunity to collect rent *twice* before the first payment is due.

If the property you plan to purchase isn't already rented, you should advertise it for rent before you've closed on the transaction. When the keys are placed in your hand, the goal is to hand them to a tenant as soon as possible, like a "hot potato."

An extra month's rent with no payments is like getting some of your down payment returned. This will increase your rate of return even higher because you'll have less of an initial investment.

One or two percent may not seem like a lot, but a few percent here and a few percent there can make a difference of *hundreds of thousands of dollars* over a long period of time.

To put this into the proper perspective, remember that the average retiree has less than $300,000 after *forty years* of saving! These little adjustments to your investment strategy can significantly increase your net worth at retirement if you start early and continue to leverage your investments to maximize their potential.

15

Performing Due Diligence

"The only real mistake is the one from which we learn nothing." –John Powell

Contract Contingencies

As a buyer, when you enter into a real estate contract, you typically would include three contingencies (conditions) that must be met or resolved before you would agree to proceed with purchasing the property. The contingencies relate to financing, appraisal, and inspection.

Financing Contingency

Prior to writing an offer to buy real estate, you must make several assumptions about your ability to secure a loan. These include the interest rate, loan term, payment amount, closing costs, and the amount of down payment that you can afford.

After you have an accepted contract with a specific loan amount and closing date, your lender can pull your credit, lock your interest rate, and give you a good faith estimate of exactly how much your loan payment and closing costs will be.

In your initial offer on a property, you indicate to the seller the loan type, amount, term, and interest rate that you intend to obtain. Most buyers cannot purchase a home without a loan, so this contingency stays in place until the sale is completed and the transaction is recorded.

If something unexpected happens that affects your ability to obtain a loan, you can cancel your contract with the seller. Such events could include being laid off unexpectedly from your job or a substantial increase in interest rate from your lender. Under these circumstances, you'd be able to have your earnest money refunded, because you had no control over your inability to meet the financing contingency.

Your earnest money might not be returned if you cause your loan to be denied because you've purchased a new car or new furniture for your house (I've seen both of these things happen). In these situations, you may lose your earnest money because your *actions* caused your loan to be declined.

The financing contingency is intended to protect the buyer if their financing falls through, but this protection *doesn't* cover stupidity!

Appraisal Contingency

Lenders require that a certified appraiser evaluate the property before they'll give you a loan. The appraisal will establish whether or not the appraiser believes the property is worth as much as you're paying for it.

Most real estate contracts provide the buyer with an opportunity to cancel the contract if the appraised value is less than the purchase price. If the appraised value is at least as much as the purchase price, the appraisal contingency is removed, and the buyer loses the right to cancel for this reason.

An appraisal contains a lot of information in addition to the appraiser's opinion of the property's value. An appraisal also includes a summary of the real estate market in the nearby area, whether prices have been rising or falling in recent months, and whether the way the property is being used is the highest and best use possible.

One recommendation I make to all of my clients is that they check the appraiser's calculation of the property's square footage (based on measuring all the exterior walls).

Be sure that the square footage on the appraisal is not significantly less than the square footage being advertised. The value of most residential property is based on the cost per square foot. If the property you're buying is smaller than

UPSIDE UP REAL ESTATE INVESTING

you've been led to believe, you could be paying tens of thousands too much!

Upside Up™ in Real Life

<u>Destroyed Equity</u>

I once purchased a property with a 500-square-foot shop in the back yard. We removed the shop, subdivided the lot, and constructed a new home where the shop had been. We failed to notice that the owner had included the shop as livable square footage because it was heated and cooled, but the appraiser would not count this as livable space because it did not have a kitchen or bathroom.

I had paid $125 per square foot for that home (and, unbeknownst to me, the shop). When the shop was demolished, I lost $62,500 (500 sq. ft. × $125/sq. ft. = $62,500). That was an expensive lesson to learn! *Read your appraisal*!

<u>Inspection Contingencies</u>

After your offer is accepted by the seller, you have a specified time period - usually ten days - in which to inspect the property. During this time, you should conduct a physical inspection, a home inspection, and a pest inspection.

Physical property inspections - After your offer has been accepted and the purchase contract has been signed by all parties, you begin a period of time known as the "inspection period." The length of time for the inspection period is negotiated in the contract.

When purchasing a single family residence, ten days is typically enough time to conduct all of the necessary inspections and research. A 500-unit apartment complex would take much longer to inspect, so an inspection period of 45 to 60 days would be necessary on a large purchase like this.

The inspection period is your opportunity to physically inspect the property and validate all of the assumptions that were made prior to making an offer on the property. During this time you must do everything possible to ensure that the property doesn't have any hidden defects.

If you discover a major defect in the property or find that the property is not a good investment, you can cancel the contract and have your earnest money refunded without the seller's approval.

If you wait until after the inspection period expires to cancel the contract, the seller must agree to release your earnest money and let you out of the contract. If the seller won't agree to let you cancel, your earnest money could be held during several months (or years) of arbitration and litigation.

A decision to cancel after the inspection period could cause the loss of your earnest money, the accumulation of huge attorney's fees, and the payment of monetary damages to the seller for breaching the contract.

Because that's a risk you probably don't wish to take, you need to inspect and validate everything you possibly can prior to the end of the inspection period.

Home inspection - Since you probably didn't take a ladder or a voltage tester with you when you were out looking at property with your REALTOR®, you'll need to conduct a home inspection. I recommend that you hire a licensed home inspector to examine every property you intend to purchase – unless you plan to tear it down.

Upside Up™ in Real Life

Home Inspections

Many people who purchase brand new homes don't hire a home inspector because the home was recently inspected by the local building inspector.

At the inspection of one client's brand new home, the inspector found that the builder had *forgotten* to install insulation in the attic!

Can you imagine how much the utility bills would have been for this home? It wouldn't take too many excessive utility bills to surpass the fee charged by the home inspector. Is this how you plan to *save* money? *Always* get an inspection, especially on brand new homes!

A home inspection will help to alleviate a lot of risk in regard to the physical condition of a property. The inspector should check the structural stability of the foundation, roof, walls, doors, and windows; test the heating and cooling system for functionality and efficiency; check the gas, electric, water, and sewer connections to verify proper operation; verify the operation and safety of major appliances, watering systems, garage door openers, and other devices; and inform you if anything is not compliant with local building codes.

This is not a place to cut corners by doing the inspection yourself or not doing one at all. A home inspection is cheap insurance against getting stuck with a "lemon" of a house. Most sellers *expect* to pay for some repairs when they accept a contract, so give them what they want! It's much easier to get the seller to pay for repairs when a certified inspector indicates that they need to be done.

Pest inspection – In Arizona, there are two kinds of homes: those that have termites and those whose owners haven't found them yet. If you live in an area that's termite-prone, a fifteen minute inspection and $50 could save you a fortune!

Upside Up™ in Real Life

<u>Termite Inspection</u>

In 2000, our termite inspector, Travis Morgan, took me into the attic of a home we had under contract. Imagine my surprise when he reached up and *snapped off a rafter!* He handed it to me, and it was as if it were made of air. The estimate to repair that home was more than $50,000 and involved removing the entire roof, rafters, and even some walls. Needless to say, Travis' company, First Inspection, has been called to inspect every home we've purchased since.

I've seen other termite inspectors drive up to a property and leave their truck running while they take a quick walk around the home. Watching them drive away without ever going inside makes me appreciate Travis even more!

Even if you live in an area that doesn't have termites, a pest control specialist can check for prior damage from pests such as carpenter ants and woodpeckers. They can also show you where you have potential health or safety problems from killer bees or rats. Both can cause serious injury or death, so again, it's worth the money to get a professional opinion.

Leases, Applications, and Rent Rolls

If you're under contract to purchase an existing rental property, you'll need to verify the financial information that the seller has provided. This includes the amount of rent, the vacancy rate, and the security deposits being held. You'll also want to find out how long the current tenants have been renting the property. In the offer, you need to ask the seller to provide the leases, applications, and rent rolls for each unit over the past two years. I usually give the seller five days from contract acceptance to provide this information to me.

Leases - The lease for each unit will provide a wealth of information, including the amount of rent being paid, the amount of the security deposit being held, the names of the people renting the property, and most importantly, the length of the lease.

A lease agreement takes precedent over a sale, so if you buy a property where the tenant has a five-year lease, you must honor the lease (and the amount of rent being charged) if the agreement was in place at the time of the sale.

If one of your assumptions was that you could raise rents or live in the unit yourself, you would not be able to do so until the lease expires or you buy the tenant out of the lease early (provided the tenant was willing to leave).

Rental application - The rental application is part of the lease and thus should be included with the lease when the owner provides a copy to you. I always review the application thoroughly because it contains a lot of information about the tenants including where they work, what kind of cars they drive, their rental history, and their Social Security numbers.

It's nice to know who you're getting into a business agreement with before you're actually in the agreement. For this reason, it may be wise to run credit and criminal background checks on the tenants who are renting the property (check with your attorney to see if this is legal in your area).

Good long-term tenants who take care of the property and don't cause problems are hard to come by. Financial stability is a desirable trait, and employment longevity has a lot to do with financial stability. Check the name of the employer listed on the rental application. When you're at the property for the inspections, ask the tenant where they work to verify that their employment hasn't changed.

Rent rolls - The rent roll is a rental history of the property. It should show the rental status of each unit during the course of the last 12 to 24 months. Verify that the vacancy loss and rents being received match the data that was provided on the real estate listing. Unexplained vacancies or other discrepancies should be explained in writing by the seller. High vacancy rates could indicate a low demand for rental property in the area.

Income Tax Returns

If the property is already being operated as a rental property, ask the seller to provide copies of their Schedule E (Form 1040) tax returns for this property for the past two tax years. The expenses listed on the seller's tax returns should be a worst case scenario of what your actual expenses will be. (Most people claim as much as they possibly can to maximize their income tax benefit). The Schedule E shows the expenses by category, such as mortgage interest, insurance, advertising, repairs, and utilities.

The reason that I always request income tax returns for the past *two years* is to ensure that the seller isn't tweaking the numbers. Some unscrupulous sellers have been known to make the previous year's income look artificially high and the expenses look unrealistically low because they knew at the time they filed their income taxes that they were going to sell the property.

Having two years of data reduces the chance of this happening, because the seller would have to know a year in advance that they were selling the property and then would have to overpay their taxes two years in a row, which is not too likely.

Dishonest people might also attempt to reduce the amount of rental income they claim on their income taxes. This is why I rely on the *leases* to determine how much *income* a property takes in, and the *tax returns* to show the property's *expenses*.

Completing Repairs

After inspecting your potential purchase as completely as possible, you'll need to determine whether any defects or conditions found during the inspections are serious enough to be "deal breakers."

Buyers typically ask the seller to repair at least some of the items that were found during the inspections, unless there are multiple offers on the property with other buyers waiting eagerly with a back-up offer.

Most homes under contract need some sort of repair. If the seller agrees to repair all of the items the buyer requests, the inspection contingency is removed. Many times the seller and buyer *negotiate* on how many of the repairs will be completed. When the negotiation is agreed upon by both the buyer and the seller, the inspection contingency is removed.

I try to include as many of the repairs as possible in the purchase contract, but we usually become aware of additional issues after all of the inspections have been completed. It's important to get quotes from contractors during the inspection period because most sellers won't agree to repair something unless they know how much it will cost.

It can sometimes take a week or more to get a quote from a contractor, so getting everything done within a ten day inspection period can sometimes be difficult. I recommend conducting the inspections as quickly as possible after the contract is accepted.

Because sellers take the path of least resistance, I try to make it easy on them by not asking them to do any of the repairs prior to closing. They're selling the property and don't care about the long-term effectiveness of the repairs. Sellers will usually purchase the cheapest materials available and will attempt to save even more money by doing the repairs themselves. This usually produces a less than optimal result with *goop* slobbered everywhere and no warranty on the work.

To keep this from happening, I schedule all of the repairs to be done *after* closing by *my* contractors. The seller pays for the repairs from their proceeds, but doesn't actually have to complete any of the work. Instead, the title company issues checks for the repairs to my contractors after the work has been done.

My contractors complete the repairs after I take ownership, so instead of substandard workmanship, I receive quality work from people who have an interest in keeping me happy (I provide them a lot of work).

The warranty on all of the completed work is in my name, rather than that of the seller, so I have no problems getting warranty items repaired. Some roof warranties are only transferable once, so why use up the warranty by transferring it from the seller to you?

If the warranty is in your name, you can transfer it to *your buyer* when you sell. This could be a selling point that causes them to choose your property over others that are for sale.

16

Confirming
Your Assumptions

"Learn from the mistakes of others. You can't live long enough to make them all yourself." –Eleanor Roosevelt (1884 - 1962)

Validating Your Assumptions

A real estate investment is the largest financial transaction that most people make in their lives. It's worth a little extra time to check prices and verify the accuracy of all the things you believe to be true about the property before you buy it. Thirty years is a long time to pay for a mistake you were *too busy* to avoid!

There's a long list of things to do during the inspection period. Because each property is different and can pose different risks, a generic list will not guarantee that everything is checked.

If you complete an *Assumption Sheet* as I suggest prior to writing the offer, you'll have a comprehensive list of every assumption that needs to be verified. As each assumption is verified, check it off your list and keep working until you've verified as many of the assumptions as possible. Your list should include all of the topics covered in this chapter.

Unit Rent

When you purchase a rental property, you must make an assumption of how much people would be willing to pay to live there. This assumption should be validated during the inspection period to ensure that your income prediction is correct.

The best way to do this is to check the rent of competing landlords. This can be done by driving around the area searching for similar properties that are available for rent. You can back up your findings by contacting a property management company to get a list of properties that are available for rent in the area and by contacting your appraiser for an estimate of market rents in the area.

CHAPTER 16 - CONFIRMING YOUR ASSUMPTIONS

Utility Usage

If you've ever been to Las Vegas, you'll understand why I don't like to pay the utility bills for tenants. When you walk around The Strip at night, you see nearly every light in every room burning bright. It's a safe bet, especially in Vegas, to assume that the nearly every room is vacant because the occupants are busy gambling in the casinos. None of these people staying at those hotels shut off the lights or turn down the air conditioning because *they* aren't paying the electricity bill.

Upside Up™ in Real Life

Paying for Water

In the early 1980s, I learned an important lesson about tenants and free utilities. The duplex I owned shared a meter between the units and I paid the bill, which averaged about $6.00 per month. Imagine my surprise when a water bill for $140 arrived in the mail!

I drove to the property, expecting to see water gushing from under the doors. Even before the tenant answered the door, I could hear the hollow *sucking* noise of water being pulled down a drain. The toilet flapper was stuck wide open and water had been constantly running down the drain for several weeks!

I asked the tenant why she hadn't noticed the noise, and she told me that she had noticed it, and that it had been so loud that she had to shut the bathroom door so she could sleep at night!

Since that day, all my leases have had a limit on the amount that I will pay for utilities.

Every time I think of the electricity being wasted in these monstrous buildings, I visualize a hotel worker stationed beside the electric meter with a grease gun. The meters are spinning so fast, they must be continually lubricated so they don't burn up! This is a visual that I don't want you to forget because tenants have the same tendency to run up the bill when you're paying for the utilities.

Upside Up™ in Real Life

Paying for Heat

In 2001, we purchased a sixteen-unit mobile home park with dilapidated 1950s trailers. All of the utilities were on a master meter, so there was no way to isolate utility usage. Although these mobile homes were less than 400 square feet in size, the utility bills in the winter averaged more than $200 per unit!

One day while working at the property, I noticed one tenant's door continually being opened and closed throughout the day. When asked why, the tenant informed me that every time it became too hot in the unit, they would open the door to cool it off.

We'd gotten an estimate of $10,000 to install separate electric meters on all the units. This incident is what made us decide to purchase the meters. We got out of the utility business and you should too!

Paying a tenant's utilities on a rental property introduces a huge risk to your profitability. You have no control over this expense, so you might as well sign a blank check and drop it off at the property each month. Utilities can drive the profitability of a property from positive to negative very quickly.

CHAPTER 16 - CONFIRMING YOUR ASSUMPTIONS

In order to get an estimate of how much the monthly utilities might cost, check the average utility expenses reported on the real estate listing sheet and also on the Schedule E tax returns. As a failsafe measure, I'd suggest calling the utility company to verify the usage history. If the utility company in your area won't provide this information, ask the seller to provide copies of the utility bills for the past year or two.

Plan to install separate utility meters for each unit as soon as possible to get out of the utility business. If the utility companies won't install the meters, or charge too much, you can have after-market sub-meters installed. You must read these meters yourself each month, but they give you the ability to bill the tenants for their utility usage.

Even if you're stuck with a lease that obligates you to pay the utilities, install the meters. When the tenants become aware that you can track how much they use, their usage will usually decrease. You can also place limits on how much you'll pay, which can't be done if you have no way to isolate the usage.

A lot of due diligence regarding utilities can be done with careful observation and common sense. Prior to purchasing, take notice of the number of electric, gas, and water meters installed on the property.

The amperage rating of the electric service should also be noted to ensure that the size is adequate to serve future electricity needs. If there is a dumpster on the property, you should assume that the owner pays for trash removal. If this expense isn't included in your assumptions, it should be added.

Insurance Cost and Claims History

The amount that the current owner pays for hazard insurance may not be the same amount your policy will cost. Insurance rates depend on the amount of coverage you have and how high you set your deductible. Contact your insurance agent and your attorney to find out the level of coverage they recommend you should carry. Your insurance company should provide a rate structure for hazard insurance at different levels of owner-paid deductibles.

Many insurance companies will also provide you with a list of things you can do to lower the cost of your insurance. These items usually involve reducing the risk for the insurance carrier. Less risk means fewer insurance claims, so the insurance companies pass some of their savings on to you.

Insurance rates are usually cheaper for owner-occupied dwellings, but don't be tempted to try and save some money by telling your agent that your child will live on the premises. Insurance is not a place to take chances by being cheap. You may be able to save $100 per year on the premium, but if the tenants decide that they don't like interior walls and remove them all, the expense to put the walls back wouldn't be covered unless you had a landlord policy.

The amount of the annual premium is tiny when compared to the cost to replace the property in the event of a major disaster or accident. Nobody ever expects catastrophes to happen to them, but bad things happen to nice people every day. Insurance is a necessary evil to protect your investment.

During the inspection period, ask the seller to provide you with an insurance claims history or CLUE report for the property. This report will show whether or not the current owner has ever made any insurance claims.

If several claims have been made on a property in the past, your insurance company may cancel your policy sometime in the future. With a history of multiple claims, it could become very difficult (and expensive) to obtain hazard insurance. This could be very serious, because insurance is a condition of your loan. Without hazard insurance, the lender will call your note due.

Upside Up™ in Real Life

<u>Allowing Pets</u>

If you're planning to allow tenants to have pets, be sure to ask your insurance agent if their company has a list of dog breeds that are not allowed to reside on the property. Our agent provided us with such a list, and I was surprised to see Chihuahuas on the roster. Apparently they're known to be just as vicious as the Rottweiler, German shepherd, and pit bull breeds, which are also on our carrier's list.

<u>Tax Assumptions</u>

You'll need to verify several assumptions about the property taxes you'll pay and income tax benefits you'll receive on the property you're considering.

Property taxes - To ensure that your property tax assumption is accurate, check with your local tax assessor's office to find out how much property taxes will be assessed for the coming year.

If taxes have not yet been assessed, get the property tax history for the past few years and calculate the percentage of the increase from previous years.

An average of the recent tax increases should provide a fairly accurate estimate of how much the new property tax might be, unless your municipality assesses taxes based upon the purchase price that's paid for a property.

Also check to see if there are any special assessments on the property. A special assessment is, in effect, a loan from the local government for recent improvements on an easement or amenity adjacent to the property, such as street lights, road work, and sidewalks.

Because many people wouldn't be able to afford all of the money up front for these improvements, the taxing authority spreads the prorated amount over several years to make it more affordable.

Income tax benefits - During the inspection period, you might want to send your income tax assumptions to your accountant to ensure that the tax refund you anticipate receiving is accurate. Your relationship with your accountant should be an ongoing one, not a once per year meeting to file income tax.

Impact of Government Restrictions

There are several assumptions related to government regulations and public services that you need to verify about the property you seek to purchase.

Local government - Go to the public works office that has jurisdiction over the property. They can provide a wealth of information that can help to mitigate many of the potential risks that come with owning real estate.

Records - Most local governments have a department that retains property records. By visiting the public records department, you can verify that all existing structures and additions have been properly permitted and built to code. If you plan to add on to existing structures, you may be required to bring those structures into compliance with current building codes.

Upside Up™ in Real Life

<u>Unpermitted Structures</u>

In 2003, we were in the process of purchasing a property with a large family room addition in the rear. Our termite inspector noticed water damage at the bottom of the paneling near the floor. Imagine our surprise when he pulled back the carpet and found *bricks!*

The addition had been built on an existing brick patio without a concrete footing or slab. Whenever it rained, the water would run from the exposed patio bricks outside, under the walls, where it was absorbed by the carpet. It was obvious that this structure was not legal or in compliance with any building codes.

Even though we'd intended to remove this structure anyway, we were able to negotiate several thousand dollars off the price. If you don't catch unpermitted structures before you purchase a property, you may be held responsible for bringing them into compliance after your purchase.

Even if you don't have plans to add on to the property, a structure built without a permit could become an issue when you attempt to sell your property at a later date.

If an unauthorized structure is discovered during the inspection period, you should attempt to make the seller remedy the problem prior to closing. Bringing the structure into compliance will ensure that you won't have to deal with it in the future.

Your title company should provide a plat map and a legal description for the property being purchased. Check with the public records department or recorder's office to see if a survey of the property has been recorded. If there seems to be confusion about a property line, I'd recommend getting a survey prior to closing on a property so you know exactly what you're buying.

Floodplain - Checking whether or not the property falls into a known floodplain will establish whether or not flood insurance is required for the property. Flood insurance can add thousands of dollars of unexpected expense each year, so it makes sense to verify whether or not you'll be required to carry this insurance.

This information can also affect your decision to purchase if you have plans to add on to the property. If the property is in a designated floodplain, you may not be able to add more square footage without hauling in tons of dirt to raise the foundation above the potential flood level. Find out what the governing agency will allow.

Upside Up™ in Real Life

<u>Property in a Floodplain</u>

In 2005, we purchased a large lot that contained three very old mobile homes. We attempted to construct new site-built homes on the property, but the city would not allow it because the property was in a floodplain.

Our hydrologist informed us that the property should no longer be in the floodplain because an eight-foot-tall culvert had been installed under a major street nearby to divert the water. Even though ten years had passed, the city never reported the change to the Federal Emergency Management Agency (FEMA).

Our hydrologist prepared a new analysis and petitioned FEMA to change the map. After several months, the map was changed and we were allowed to subdivide and build on the property. The neighboring properties also benefited from our efforts. Nearly fifty other homes were also removed from the floodplain and no longer required flood insurance!

Wastewater - The wastewater department can verify whether or not the property is connected to a sanitary sewer system. Many people don't want to worry about a septic system, and may not consider buying a property that isn't connected to a municipal sewer system.

If you intend to build on the property, wastewater officials in your city or county may be able to provide maps that show where active and abandoned septic tanks and their associated drain fields are located. They can also provide the location and depths of sewer pipes in the street.

This information could prove to be useful if you decide to build additional structures on the property. Gravity is needed to make the sewage flow properly, so you'll need to know the distance between the structure and the street to calculate the vertical drop.

Zoning - Zoning ordinances usually regulate things like building height, setbacks from property lines (on the front, rear, and sides of parcels), land coverage ratios (for buildings, sidewalks, driveways, and detached structures), intended usage for each zoning class (i.e., residential or commercial), and minimum lot size.

Even if you have no plans to build on the property, zoning should be taken into account. The *ability* to build on or split the parcel can make a huge difference in the value when you sell later on.

Deed Restrictions and HOAs

Be sure to check for deed restrictions or homeowners' association rules and regulations that might affect the investment potential of the property you are evaluating.

Deed restrictions - Deed restrictions are usually established when a property is initially subdivided. Created by the developer or subdivider of the property, the deed restrictions establish rules for the neighborhood that are usually much more restrictive than zoning ordinances. Be sure to obtain a copy of the recorded deed restrictions to ensure that the subdivision rules don't prohibit anything that you plan to do.

As the property changes ownership, new owners can attach more restrictions on the parcels that they own.

Upside Up™ in Real Life

<u>Deed Restrictions</u>

My wife and I constructed a new home on a vacant lot next to our home. Prior to selling the property, we added a height restriction that prohibits any structure over 12-feet tall from being constructed.

This restriction will protect the views of the mountains that we enjoy from our home across the adjacent lot. We also placed a restriction specifying the distance that a garage or other structure must be from our property line to keep future owners from building too close to us.

Because we own the property now, we can control its use in the future, as long as our requirements comply with zoning ordinances, existing deed restrictions, and state or federal laws. You must be careful, however, not to limit a property's future use to the extent that you'll have difficulty selling it.

Homeowners' associations - Homeowners' associations (HOAs) create sets of rules known as *CC&Rs*, which stands for covenants, conditions, and restrictions. CC&Rs are intended to preserve property values in the neighborhood. These rules are similar to deed restrictions.

These covenants, conditions, and restrictions are usually more limiting than either zoning regulations or deed restrictions. Homeowners' associations collect membership dues to pay for managing the association, which includes enforcing the CC&Rs.

223

If the property you're purchasing has a homeowners' association, read a copy of the CC&Rs during the inspection period to ensure that the rules aren't too restrictive.

Sometimes these associations can backfire when overzealous neighbors are allowed to disregard common sense in their efforts to enforce the rules. In a neighborhood where we once lived, the covenants stated that a garage door could not be open for more than 15 minutes. One neighbor would sit outside with a stop watch to ensure that everyone complied.

Obviously, the rule was intended to discourage people from keeping their garage doors open all day long. But, because of the way the rule was written, one *idiot* was allowed to use the rule for some sort of power play.

A well-managed association can raise property values because it can ensure that people are not storing junk or parking old cars in their yards. But, some parts of the CC&Rs may affect your decision to buy. If you're considering the purchase of a property as a rental, verify during the inspection period that the property can be rented to tenants (this practice is not allowed by some associations).

Before you make plans to alter paint colors, find out whether the HOA requires special paint. We once had a house 90% painted with an approved color before the HOA informed us that the *reflectivity* of the paint was higher than they would allow. To appease the association, we had to repaint our home with paint that had a lower reflectivity rating. This substantially increased our cost and the time required to complete the job.

If you plan to allow your renters to have pets in your property, contact the HOA president or the management company to find out if there are rules governing pets in the neighborhood. While speaking with the HOA representative, verify the amount of the current association dues, and whether there are any plans to raise the dues in the near future.

In the event you decide to add on to your property, ask about the process that must be followed for the association to approve the additions you plan to make. The most important question to ask is whether any major improvements are planned for the neighborhood.

Upside Up™ in Real Life

HOA Improvements

Asking the HOA whether there are any major improvements planned for the neighborhood could save you thousands of dollars, as it did for us during the purchase of one home.

The HOA bookkeeper informed us that the roads in the entire neighborhood were being resurfaced by the county and each home in the subdivision was being charged $2,200 to pay for the work.

If I hadn't asked, we would not have known about the $2,200 until after we had closed. Because I found out during the inspection period, we were able to get the sellers to pay the $2,200 fee at closing.

Paying this unexpected road fee would have significantly changed the return on investment (ROI) for this property. If we would have had to pay for the road resurfacing, our initial investment would have been more than ten percent higher!

17

Modifying
Your Mindset

"The only limit to our realization of tomorrow will be our doubts of today. Let us move forward with strong and active faith." –Franklin Delano Roosevelt

A Summary of What You've Learned

This is the book about real estate investment I wish someone else had written before I started investing twenty-five years ago. If I could have benefited from the experiences of others, I could have saved making a lot of mistakes.

I'm pleased to be sharing this book with you now. It's based on the successes I've had and the mistakes I've made during the past twenty-five years of investing in real estate.

I call it the *Upside Up* ™ system for real estate investment, and here's what I hope you've been able learn from it.

You should realize the many benefits of owning investment property and have several ideas you can implement to minimize your investment, lower your risk, increase your profitability, and return your investment capital quickly.

You should know how to locate, analyze, inspect, and finance the properties that match your tenants' needs.

You should understand that wealth from real estate investments can help you achieve financial freedom, and that you owe it to yourself and your family to achieve the highest standard of living possible.

How to Get Started

You cannot make a difference in your life and in the lives of others if you live paycheck to paycheck, spending all that you earn as fast as you receive it.

For some people in this situation, it might seem as if there's no way to change the condition or outcome of their lives. It's very easy to lose all hope and become a victim of self-pity. Under these circumstances, many people just give up and stop trying.

CHAPTER 17 - MODIFYING YOUR MINDSET

If this is where you are, you need to *SHOCK!!* your system by directing your focus away from yourself and onto those who are less fortunate than you. You'll notice a miraculous transformation in your attitude as you to realize how blessed you are compared to others in the world.

Instead of complaining about the things you *don't* have, you'll become thankful for the things that you *do* have. This realization will change your focus from internal to external and you'll begin to see encouraging opportunities rather than impossible difficulties. In life, your *attitude* determines the *altitude* you rise to.

Once you begin to realize the possibility of doing better, you can create goals for yourself. Nothing you do at a job working for others can replace the sense of accomplishment you feel from doing something for yourself or your family. Something that *you* think of, *you* work at, and *you* accomplish can never be taken away from you.

The more you experience this feeling of accomplishment, the easier it becomes to repeat the process again and again. When you start stacking one success upon another, your confidence takes over and success becomes something you do automatically rather than something you have to work at.

Many people are afraid to fly on an airplane because of some well-publicized plane crashes. Statistics show that far more people are killed in automobiles each year than die in airplanes, even as a percentage, but still the mind sees what it has been programmed to see.

You'll have to look hard to find your own inadvertent beliefs and reflex actions that are stopping you from achieving your dreams. What keeps many people from being successful is the fear of failure. This is so ironic because without taking action, you don't just have a *chance* to fail, you're *guaranteed* to fail!

I recommend these four steps to overcome your fear of investing in real estate:

1) take self-improvement classes

2) join an investor club

3) make a public proclamation

4) find the right real estate agent

Self-improvement Classes

Community colleges offer an array of self-improvement learning opportunities, including classes in self-defense, foreign languages, investment, and financial management. I recommend taking as many of these classes as you can afford and have the time to take. The inspiration to complete this book came from classes I took at Pima Community College in Tucson, Arizona.

Since 2001, I've been paid to teach college classes on investing and prior to that, I volunteered for many years with the Junior Achievement program, teaching personal finance to sixth and seventh-grade students.

After nearly twenty years of teaching, I can honestly say that I've never taught a class in which I didn't also learn something. Even though I'm paid to teach classes and mentor my real estate clients, I do it because of the continuous education that *I* receive from my students.

Each person you come into contact with will have a different approach to solving the problems they encounter. If you're associated with a variety of people, you'll discover a variety of ideas. The more ideas you have, the better decisions you'll be able to make.

Investor Clubs

Real estate investor clubs can be found in most large cities. Besides offering member discounts at various local businesses, most investor clubs provide ongoing educational opportunities.

Upside Up™ in Real Life

Join an Investor Club

When a new club for real estate investors was being started in Tucson, I was intrigued enough to join. At each monthly meeting for the past four years, the Arizona Real Estate Investor's Association (AZREIA) has had a different speaker on such topics as foreclosure sales, tax liens, and wholesaling.

I can't remember attending a single meeting of AZREIA at which I didn't learn something. No matter how much experience you have, you'll benefit from spending time around other investors who are active in your market

About once per year, we have a session called "The good, the bad, and the ugly". This is an excellent opportunity to learn from the mistakes and triumphs other people have made with their investments.

All that is necessary for these meetings is an open mind and a notepad. For information on AZREIA, you can visit their website at <azreia.org>. If you're in another state, check your area for a similar organization. The discounts offered by local businesses to members should more than offset the cost of dues.

These clubs often invite different speakers each month to inform the club members of new investment strategies. Sometimes the speakers are from the local area, and other times they're national speakers who are selling a specific type of investment system that they've mastered.

Whether you buy their systems or not, I recommend that you go to each meeting to get new ideas and to network with other like-minded individuals in your local area.

The other investors in the club should not be viewed as your competition just because they're trying to accomplish the same investment goals that you are. Many investments require partnering with others.

Surrounding yourself with a network of like-minded people will build a support group that can be instrumental in helping you achieve your goals. When the people in your peer group begin to invest, it will give you the courage to do it too.

Public Proclamation

Our pride is a huge motivator to accomplish what we set out to do. Whenever I've taken on a challenging task, I tell everyone that I know what I plan to do.

Public proclamations are responsible for helping me to achieve many of my toughest goals. I compiled information for this book for nearly five years, but never found the time to actually write it. In 2006, I announced to all of my friends and family in my Christmas letter that I was going to finish my book in the following year. The public challenge I made to myself was successful, because you're reading about it now!

When you make a public proclamation, pay attention to how the people around you respond to the news. This is a good way of determining who your true friends are. Those who are small-minded or jealous of your accomplishments may be afraid that you're going to pass them in social status.

They won't be supportive of your goals and will privately hope that you fail. Because these people have never had the courage to change their own situation, your success will make them feel like a failure.

Don't let these people get you down. Surround yourself with genuine friends who have positive attitudes and are supportive of your ambitions. True friends will help you to succeed at your endeavors. Their encouragement will lift your spirits and increase your commitment to follow through and complete what you set out to do.

The Right Real Estate Agent

By now, you've probably gotten some innovative ideas of how to create value in your local real estate market. Before you start looking at properties, you need to locate a REALTOR® in your area who specializes in investment property and actively invests in the local real estate market.

Many people have the mistaken belief that a real estate agent who also invests is going to keep all of the good deals for themselves. It's nearly impossible for one investor to affect the market.

About twenty-thousand properties are sold each year in my community of Tucson, Arizona. Do you really think that the few parcels I purchase each year make a dent in the supply?

If so, you need to change your belief system from seeing the world as a glass *half empty* (limited supply) and begin to see the glass as *half full* (unlimited supply).

If you believe that there is a limited supply of anything, than a shortage might as well exist. The limit that exists in your mind is projected upon everything you see whether it's really there or not. You'll *never* find deals if you don't believe there are any! Keeping an open mind will create unlimited possibilities.

Upside Up™ in Real Life

<u>Get a Coach</u>

The average real estate agent spends a good deal of their time and money looking for customers. In the "information age" that we live in, I can't believe that there are still brokers who hand a new real estate agent a telephone directory and say, "start calling."

Since joining Craig Proctor's *Quantum Leap* coaching program <www.quantumleapsystem.com>, my wife and I have been able to totally transform our real estate business. We no longer *look* for customers; *they call us* because of the unique programs Craig Proctor developed and has shared with his students for many years.

During the housing market downturn in 2007, our company sold more homes with *three* agents than we'd been able to sell during the market "high" in 2005 with *eighteen* agents!

You need to work *smarter*, not *harder!* Find someone who's done what you want to do and ask them for help. Whatever they charge will be well worth it, it certainly was for us!

One of the biggest reasons to utilize the services of an investor/agent is that they already have a team of contractors in place. If you buy your properties from someone who invests themselves, they'll gladly share the names of the key team members that you'll need to become successful. Starting out with the right contractors will save both time and money.

In order to learn, you *must* make mistakes. Throughout this book, I've shared several of the investing mistakes that I've made during the past twenty-five years. Believe me; any experienced investor/agent has made plenty of mistakes themselves. They can add to my list and help you to avoid repeating the same mistakes that *they've* made.

There's a big difference between theory and practice. How much can you learn from someone who has never done what you want to accomplish? I'd much rather be *shown* what works than *told* what *might* work.

When interviewing prospective real estate agents, ask how many investment properties they sell each year and how many they buy themselves. Ask them what their investment strategy is (buy and hold, fix and flip, build and sell, etc.)

If their strategy depends on market appreciation, find someone else to represent you! You need a system that is fast, profitable, repeatable, and doesn't depend upon market appreciation.

That's been my motivation for developing, teaching, and now writing about the *Upside Up*™ system.

Happy Investing!

Bob Zachmeier

INDEX

INDEX

UPSIDE UP REAL ESTATE INVESTING

ABOUT THE AUTHOR

Bob Zachmeier is an entrepreneur, investor, lecturer, author, and self-made millionaire. Born and raised in Mandan, North Dakota, his parents taught by example that a strong work ethic and determination could achieve almost any goal.

As the third of six children, Zachmeier learned early in life to become self-reliant. At the age of sixteen, he owned a fireworks business, complete with billboard and radio advertising, which helped fund his college education and that of several of his siblings.

He first invested in real estate in 1982 at the age of twenty-two. After several years of losing with the "buy-and-pray" strategy used by many beginning investors, he developed a system to *create* wealth rather than depend upon the real estate market for his success.

Within a few years of employing this new system, he was earning enough money through real estate investments to leave his job and end a twenty-two-year career in the electronics industry. Since that time, he has fine-tuned his investment process into the *Upside Up*™ system it is today.

After more than two decades of real estate investing, Zachmeier and his wife, Camille, saw the need to share what they'd learned with others. In 2004, they founded *Win3 Realty*, a successful real estate company in Tucson, Arizona, to help homeowners and beginning investors achieve success and avoid costly mistakes.

By sharing his experiences and practical investment advice as real estate broker, coach, college teacher, and author, Bob Zachmeier has helped thousands of people improve their financial well-being.

To learn more about the *Upside Up*™ system, including additional titles in the *Upside Up*™ book series, visit the publisher's website at <www.outoftheboxbooks.com>. Or contact the author via e-mail at <bob@bobzachmeier.com>.

Printed in the United States
122670LV00003B/82/P